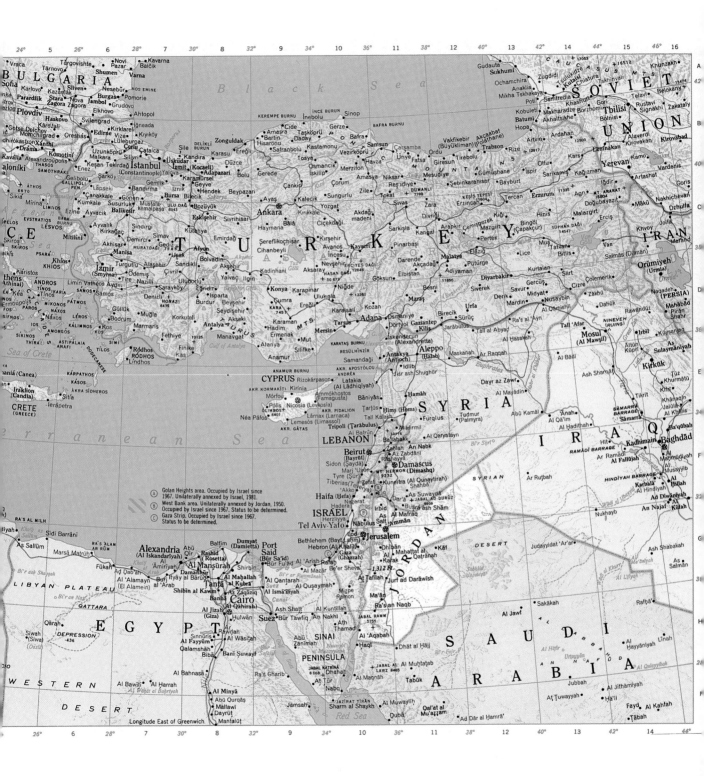

Enchantment of the World

LEBANON

By Leila Merrell Foster

Consultant for Lebanon: Bernard Reich, Ph.D., Professor, Department of Political Science, George Washington University, Washington, D.C.

Consultant for Reading: Robert L. Hillerich, Ph.D., Visiting Professor, University of South Florida; Consultant, Pinellas County Schools, Florida

CHILDRENS PRESS®

CHICAGO

Lebanon, on the shores of the Mediterranean Sea

Project Editor: Mary Reidy
Design: Margrit Fiddle

Library of Congress Cataloging-in-Publication Data

Foster, Leila Merrell.
    Lebanon / by Leila M. Foster.
        p.   cm. — (Enchantment of the world)
    Includes index.
    Summary: Describes the geography, history, culture,
industry, and people of Lebanon.
    ISBN 0-516-02601-1
    1. Lebanon—Juvenile literature.   [1. Lebanon.]
I. Title. II. Series.
DS80.F67 1992   91-32230
956.92—dc20   CIP
                                                                        AC

Picture Acknowledgments
AP/Wide World Photos: 11, 54 (right), 58 (2 photos), 59, 61 (2 photos), 62 (2 photos), 66 (3 photos), 68, 69 (right), 70, 72, 73 (2 photos), 75, 76, 77, 92 (bottom right)
H. Armstrong Roberts: © M. Spector, 12 (right)
Historical Pictures Service: 46 (left)
Nawrocki Stock Photo: © Imapress/Granet, 8 (left); © Imapress/Philiptchenko, 92 (top); © Imapress/Coudreau, 104 (bottom)
North Wind Picture Archives: 31 (2 photos), 33 (3 photos), 35 (right), 41, 46 (right)
Photri: 4, 5, 10, 13 (left), 14 (bottom), 19, 20, 21, 22 (bottom right), 29 (left), 38, 86, 102 (top), 105, 106 (2 photos); © Lehtikuva Oy, 69 (left), 92 (bottom left)
© **Carl Purcell:** 83, 87 (left), 98 (left)
Root Resources: © Irene E. Hubbell, 24 (bottom)
SuperStock International, Inc.: © World Photo Svc. Ltd., Cover, 8 (right), 16, 18, 85; © Charles Bear, 6 (bottom); © Maynard Williams, 7, 78, 82; © William L. Hamilton, 22 (left); © Peter Schmid, 84; © Kurt Scholz, 88, 97, 123; © G. Ricatto, 90 (top)
TSW-CLICK/Chicago: © Bill Staley, 107
Valan: © Christine Osborne, 6 (top), 12 (left), 13 (right), 22 (top right), 29 (right), 52 (bottom), 87 (right), 90 (bottom), 94, 95 (2 photos), 96, 98 (right), 99, 100 (2 photos), 101, 102 (bottom), 104 (top left and right), 109; © Kennon Cooke, 17
Len W. Meents: Maps on 14 (top), 24 (top), 28, 32, 34, 35 (left), 37, 45, 47, 49, 52 (top), 54 (left), 57
Courtesy Flag Research Center, Winchester, Massachusetts 01890: Flag on back cover
Cover: View of city and harbor, Beirut, Lebanon

A view of Tripoli, with the ruins of a Crusader fortress in the background

TABLE OF CONTENTS

Shoppers seem to ignore the damaged buildings in Beirut as they go about their business (inset). Pigeon Grotto on the coast of Beirut (below)

A cedar tree

Chapter 1

WAR-TORN PARADISE AND ITS PEOPLE

What is it like to live in a country on the shores of the blue Mediterranean Sea? What is it like to live in a country with towering snow-covered mountain peaks, sparkling springs of water, and ancient stands of cedar trees and other forests? What is it like to live in a country where gunfire and rockets disturb people's sleep? What is it like to live in a country where people may be kidnapped and brutally beaten or killed? What is it like to live in a country where neighbors fight against neighbors, and where world powers invade from outside? These questions can be put to the Lebanese because they live in a country of great beauty and great conflict.

Lebanon is situated on the eastern coast of the Mediterranean Sea. Its borders are shared with Israel to the south and with Syria to the east and north. At the western edge of Asia, Lebanon is a narrow strip of land about 120 miles (193 kilometers) from north to south and 50 miles (80 kilometers) from east to west.

Ruins from the Umayyad Dynasty (above) date from the eighth century. Twentieth-century Lebanese youths proudly display their country's flag (left).

Approximately three million people live in an area of 4,015 square miles (10,399 square kilometers) — smaller than the state of Connecticut.

There is no official religion; the country is home to people of many religions. Arabic is the official language. The flag has three stripes: red on the top and bottom, and white in the center. A green cedar tree, for which the country has been famous throughout history, is on the center white stripe.

Lebanon is home to some of the oldest human settlements in the world. The area has been the base for world civilizations. Yet in modern history Lebanon is counted as one of the newer nations, just having achieved its independence in 1943, although French troops remained until 1946. Lebanon has been called the "Playground of the Middle East" because of the recreational advantages of the sea and the mountains. Lebanon also has been the leading center for trade and financial services in the Middle

East. The country was torn apart with civil war that began in 1975. Although there was a cease-fire in 1976, fighting continues.

There are internal problems that have hurt the country's economy. Lebanon was invaded by Israel in 1982. The country has been the pawn in the power politics of nations such as Syria, Iraq, and Iran—neighbors in the Middle East.

Lebanon has struggled to stay alive as one country. The fighting among many small groups, often supported by foreign forces, made it difficult to achieve truces—much less lasting peace.

Throughout history the area of present-day Lebanon has had strategic importance. Its mountains and valleys have provided a refuge for victims of oppression and have fostered an independent spirit in its people. It is not surprising then that the population should be composed of numerous ethnic and religious groups that include descendants of the Phoenicians, the Greeks, the Romans, the Byzantines, and the Crusaders, plus people from the Arabian Peninsula, Armenians, and, most recently, Palestinians. After Israel became a state in 1948, an estimated 270,000 Palestinians crossed the southern border of Lebanon and now live in Lebanon as refugees. Each of these groups brought a religion and a culture; and each has had an influence on the present population of Lebanon.

When the boundaries of Greater Lebanon were drawn after World War I, the population was predominantly Christian. Today, the balance has shifted so that there are more Muslims. This is due to larger Muslim families and to the number of Palestinians currently living in Lebanon. However, within each faith group there are differences that play an important role resulting in Christians opposing Christians and Muslims fighting Muslims as well as the Christian-Muslim conflicts.

A Maronite church in Bsharri

CHRISTIANS

Among the Christians there are several groups called Uniate Catholics. They recognize the authority of the Roman Catholic pope, but have their own form of worship; in some instances, they have a married clergy. These groups are the Maronites, Greek Catholics (Melkites), and Armenian Catholics. Other Christian groups are Roman Catholic, Armenian (Gregorian) Orthodox, Greek Orthodox, Nestorian Assyrian, and Protestant.

The largest number of Lebanese Christians are Maronites. The Maronites, who had a different idea of the nature of Christ than other Christians, sought refuge in the seventh century A.D. in present-day Lebanon. They were being persecuted by the Byzantine government that had its capital in present-day Turkey.

Although the Maronites entered into partial communion with the Roman Catholic church at the time of the Crusades in the twelfth century A.D., 1763 is the date of their full communion with that church. They have aligned themselves with the West and have especially close ties with France.

Shiite Muslim women

The Greek Orthodox, who are Arab, recognize the *patriarch* (leader) in Damascus, Syria. They live in many parts of the Middle East, unlike the Maronites who are concentrated in Lebanon. The Armenian Catholics and the Armenian Orthodox sought refuge in Lebanon after the Armenian massacres by the Turks during and after World War I. They speak the Armenian language and have a non-Arab background.

MUSLIMS

The two main branches of Islam, the Sunnis and the Shiites, are represented in Lebanon. They differ in their understanding of how religious leaders should be chosen and in their interpretation of the law and practices of their faith in their own communities.

The Sunnis are the larger segment of Muslims in most of the countries in which the Arabs settled. However, the Shiites, made up of native-born Lebanese and persons coming more recently from Iran, outnumber the Sunnis in Lebanon.

11

Above: Palestinian refugees live in makeshift dwellings.
Left: A member of the Druze faith, known as Muwahiddun

DRUZE

The Druze were originally Muslim and then converted to the teachings of a Shiite leader and developed their own individuality in the eleventh century. They prefer to be known as *Muwahiddun*. They keep their faith secret, reject converts, and marry within their group.

FRAGMENTED LEBANESE

Refugees who fled from Palestine at the time of the formation of the state of Israel in 1948, from Jordan in 1970, and later Syria are mostly Sunni Muslims, along with some Christians. Many live in shabby areas and want to return to their homes outside Lebanon. All of these different groups are separated by language or accents, dress, religious faith, and customs. They seem to have developed a more intense loyalty to their own people than to the nation of Lebanon. In times of conflict some of the groups have formed their own militia for defense and attack. However, economic and

*There was a time in Lebanon when people could
gather along the seacoast to chat and relax (left), and
some people enjoyed themselves at the Yacht Club (right) in Beirut.*

political self-interest has encouraged these diverse people to work together at certain periods of the history of the nation.

For centuries, the Lebanese have been the most Westernized people in the Arab world. Lebanese adaptations of Western ideas continue to affect the rest of the Arab world.

CONCERN FOR LEBANON

There has been real concern that the nation of Lebanon may self-destruct and break into fragments or be swallowed up by outsiders. Certainly, foreign countries have tried to control the destiny of Lebanon, and foreign countries are still maneuvering in the power politics of the Middle East and the world.

It is hoped that one day Lebanon will again become the peaceful playground of the Middle East and attract travelers from the desert countries of the Middle East and from all parts of the world. Then Lebanese and their visitors will enjoy the natural beauty of the sea and mountains and the cultural opportunities that are part of the heritage of Lebanon.

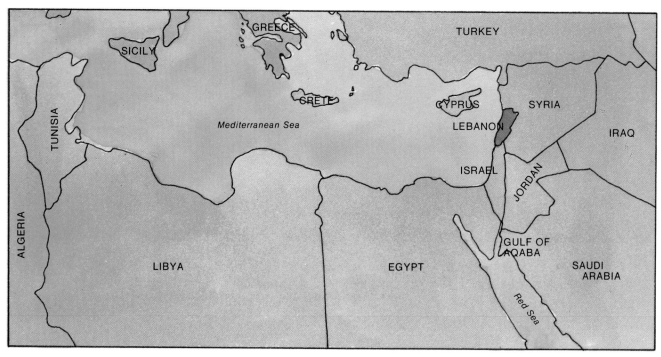

Above: Lebanon, which appears in orange, is one of many countries that has access to the Mediterranean Sea. Below: It took generations to complete these terraces on the mountain slopes.

Chapter 2

LAND OF SEACOAST, MOUNTAINS, VALLEYS, AND TREES

Just as Lebanon is made up of many peoples, so also the country's physical features, climate, soils, water supply, and plant and animal life are greatly varied. The four geographical areas are the coastal plain, the coastal mountain range (Lebanon Mountains), the central plateau or valley (Bekaa Valley), and the interior mountain range (Anti-Lebanon Mountains). Each of these areas has differences in climate, soil and minerals, water supply, vegetation and animal life, and population settlements.

THE COASTAL PLAIN

Because Lebanon borders the east coast of the Mediterranean Sea, the principal cities are located in this area. Sea routes provided transportation and communication in ancient times and Lebanon's coast was the home of the ancient Phoenicians, a great seafaring people. There are few good natural harbors, but many shallow and curved bays. People often built cities on islands or

Ancient ruins at Tyre

rocky promontories that were easier to defend. The Phoenician seaport of Tyre was built on an island separated from the mainland by a channel.

The coastal plain is narrow. At its widest point in the north along the Syrian border it is about eight miles (thirteen kilometers), and forms the Akkar Plain. At other points, the coastal plain is interrupted where the mountains come down to the sea. Rocky beaches and sandy bays can be found. Rivers emptying into the sea have deposited soil that is generally fertile.

Along the coast, the summers are hot and humid with little or no rain. Heavy dews provide moisture for agriculture in the area. West winds bring a cooling during the afternoon and evening, while at night the direction is reversed and the wind blows out to sea. Storms that form over the Mediterranean bring rain in winter, but heavy rainfall lasts only a few days, and the amount of rainfall varies greatly. Sometimes there are frosts during the

Flamingos

winter when cold winds blow in from Europe, and about once
every fifteen years a light snow falls as far south as Beirut.

Hot winds blowing from the Egyptian deserts provide a
warming trend more often in the spring than in the fall. The
Lebanese call these winds *shuluq*, which means "splitter" or
"cleaver." An east wind, also dry and hot, from the Indian Ocean
reaches Lebanon. It is called *sharqiyah*, or "eastern." Rarely lasting
more than three days, this wind can bring violent sandstorms.
Along the coast the sea moderates temperature extremes.

Migratory birds from Africa and Europe such as flamingos,
pelicans, cormorants, ducks, herons, and snipes are found in the
marshes. Marine life does not thrive in the eastern part of the
Mediterranean because the waters there do not have good
nutrients. Some species of fish are caught in small numbers.
Mosquitoes that carry malaria are a special problem around the
Akkar Plain near Tripoli.

Farmlands near Baalbek, with Jabal Sannin in the background

THE COASTAL MOUNTAIN RANGE

The Lebanon Mountains rise abruptly from the coastal plain. The range runs the length of the coast, diminishing in height from north to south, and merges into the hills of Galilee. The highest peaks are around Bsharri, southeast of Tripoli. Qurnat as-Sawda is the highest at 10,115 feet (3,083 meters); a peak northeast of Beirut is Jabal Sannin at 8,557 feet (2,608 meters).

An unusual geological feature of the up fold of the Lebanon Mountains that does not exist in the same range in either Syria or Israel is a layer of nonporous rocks that forces considerable quantities of water to the surface in the form of springs. These springs can be found at the unusual height of 3,937 feet to 4,921 feet (1,200 meters to 1,500 meters). Some of the springs have a

River water cultivates land on the western side of the mountains.

strong flow and form small rivers. These rivers water the western side of the mountains and, with irrigated terraces, make cultivation of crops possible at higher levels. Other rivers on the western slopes that are not spring fed may be seasonal—running only during the rainy winter months. There is one seasonal lake fed by springs on the eastern slopes near Yammunah, 25 miles (40 kilometers) southeast of Tripoli.

Temperatures are cooler at the height of 5,000 feet (1,524 meters) where the highest settlements are located. From December to May, the higher mountains are covered with snow. More than 60 inches (152 centimeters) of precipitation fall in the higher altitudes. During peace time, skiing was the highlight of the winter sports season, while the summer months attracted people to the mountain resorts.

During ancient and medieval times, the country was heavily forested. The cedars on the slopes of the Lebanon Mountains were especially sought for buildings and ships. In the Bible King Solomon's palace is called "the house of the Forest of Lebanon"

19

The trees of the Lord are watered abundantly,
  the cedars of Lebanon which he planted.
In them the birds build their nests;
  the stork has her home in the fir trees.
The high mountains are for the wild goats;
  the rocks are a refuge for the badgers.
Thou hast made the moon to mark the seasons;
  the sun knows its time for setting.
Thou makest darkness, and it is night,
  when all the beasts of the forest creep forth.
The young lions roar for their prey,
  seeking their food from God.
When the sun rises, they get them away
  and lie down in their dens.
Man goes forth to his work
  and to his labor until the evening.
(Psalms 104: 16-23.)

A stand of cedar trees on a barren hill

(I Kings 7:2). Now, however, there are only a few groves of cedars that are protected as the symbol of Lebanon. Because so much of the natural vegetation was cut, burned, and grazed for so long, only brush and low trees such as oaks, pines, cypresses, firs, junipers, and carobs grow now. Where they still stand, some of the cedars have grown over eighty feet (twenty-four meters) tall and are estimated to be one thousand years old.

Today bears and wildcats are sometimes seen in the mountains. Smaller animals include deer, hedgehogs, squirrels, martens, dormice, and hares. Eagles, buzzards, kites, falcons, and hawks live in the mountains. Owls, kingfishers, cuckoos, and woodpeckers are common also.

The Litani River flows through the Bekaa Valley.

THE CENTRAL PLATEAU OR VALLEY

The mountains separate the Bekaa Valley from the sea. In the valley there is less precipitation and humidity than on the coastal plain. A wider variation in temperature also occurs during the day and throughout the year. More snow falls here than at comparable altitudes to the west. The valley receives fifteen to twenty-five inches (thirty-eight to sixty-four centimeters) of precipitation annually.

The valley is from 6 to 16 miles (10 to 26 kilometers) wide and is an extension of the East African Rift Valley. Toward the south the valley becomes hilly as it blends into the foothills of Mt. Hermon. The Litani River is 90 miles (145 kilometers) long and begins near Baalbek. It then flows south through the valley to end in the sea near Tyre. The Orontes River is called the *Nahr al-Asi,*

Above: Fresh produce in a Lebanon market
Above right: Harvesting wheat
Right: A shepherd with his flock of sheep

"Rebel" River in Arabic, because of its unusual direction. It reaches the Mediterranean after it flows north through Syria and Turkey.

Wild wheat and barley grow in this valley, and it is in a place like this that humans first learned to cultivate the crops that are ground to make flour for bread. Today wheat, barley, maize, lentils, peas, onions, garlic, cucumbers, tomatoes, potatoes, and tobacco are grown in this area. Herbs and medicinal plants are found here also. Forage for animals is cultivated, and chickens, goats, sheep, cows, asses, mules, and horses are common farm animals.

INTERIOR MOUNTAIN RANGE

The Bekaa Valley separates the Lebanon Mountains from the Anti-Lebanon Mountains, the interior mountain range along the eastern border with Syria. This interior zone of mountains and *steppe* (plains with few trees) has less rainfall than the coastal mountains. Because of the height of this land, it gets more precipitation in the form of snow. This range is famous for snow-covered Mt. Hermon in the south (9,232 feet; 2,814 meters).

Once this range was thickly forested, but much has been cut for fuel and building materials. The Arabic word *jurud*, meaning "stripped" or "barren," has been applied to the high regions because of the deforestation. The demand for wood from neighboring countries lacking this resource has always been so great that the forests have been endangered. Sixty percent of the trees of Lebanon were cut during World War I—primarily by the Turks who used the timber for railroads. However, the British and French also used wood from Lebanon during World War II for a coastal railroad. Now only juniper bushes, bunch grass, and cactus grow in many areas. At higher elevations, there are stunted trees, bushes, and small flowers.

It is the variety of the geographical conditions within the country that has shaped the history of Lebanon and given it much of its beauty. The sea has provided an outlet for expansion and exploration. The land with its coastal path formed the bridge, and sometimes the battleground, for great empires. Snow-covered mountains and the rich forests attracted desert dwellers. In a wood-poor part of the world, the forests encouraged both trade and conquest. All these helped to form a people in whom diversity and independence were likely to thrive.

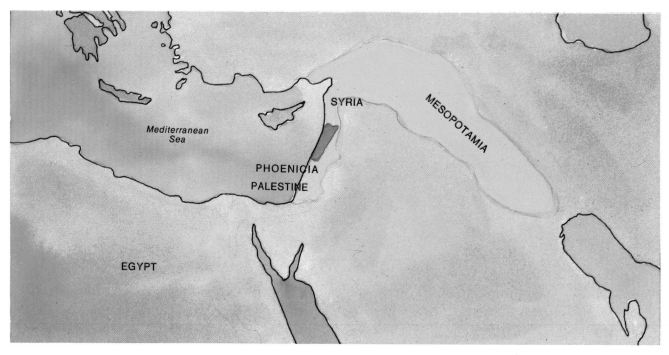

*Above: The area the Phoenicians inhabited   Lebanon of
today is shown in orange.*
Below: Remains of the Phoenician harbor at Byblos

Chapter 3

ANCIENT LEBANON

The great seafaring and trading nation of Phoenicia arose in the area that is now called Lebanon about 1200 B.C., but there was a historic and even prehistoric occupation of Lebanon before that. The Phoenicians both continued and changed the culture that existed before their appearance. Many other great civilizations also have left their imprint on this land.

BEFORE WRITTEN HISTORY

The earliest archaeological evidence of human habitation of the area comes from the city of Byblos (now Jubayl). As early as 5000 B.C., the largest Neolithic settlement in the Mediterranean area existed on these heights near the sea. The people who lived here farmed, raised sheep, and fished. Production of woven goods and yarns that was to be characteristic of Byblos and the Phoenicians is present even in this earliest of times. Pottery has been discovered in this same area. This pottery is decorated with impressions of the backs of shells in the clay or hand-drawn triangles in a herringbone pattern. Also, pebbles have been found with the carvings of figures of deities (gods and goddesses).

During the Copper Age, between 4000 and 3000 B.C., contacts with the Mesopotamian civilizations from the east between the Tigris and Euphrates rivers must have been made because there is a similarity between objects produced in the two areas. For example, an ivory carving of a four-footed animal on the front of a jar is very similar to one found in Ur (in present-day Iraq). This is the earliest example of the craft of ivory carving that was to be associated with the Phoenicians.

THE URBAN REVOLUTION

A revolution of sorts took place around 3000 B.C. as groups of buildings—sanctuaries, homes, and public structures—formed what could be called cities. This "urban revolution" was located along the coastline. Byblos again is the site where the development began, and this spot was a natural trading station on the routes along the coast between Egypt, Palestine, Syria, and Mesopotamia.

Egypt was its most important trading partner and influenced the culture of Byblos. Traders from the delta area of the Nile River in Egypt came to Byblos for timber, metals, and other goods. Around 2600 B.C. there was even an Egyptian temple in the city.

During a period of internal unrest in Egypt that prevented trade with Byblos, the Egyptians lamented the fact that no one was sailing to Byblos for the cedar for their mummy cases. The beautiful mummy cases and the temple doors in Egypt had been made from the cedars of Lebanon.

Byblos also traded with cities to the north. Written documents on clay tablets found at the city of Ebla (now in present-day Syria) give evidence of the economic power of Byblos. Byblos imported crude metals, textiles, perfumes, livestock, and food while exporting articles made of linen and finished metal products. A princess of Ebla became the wife of a king of Byblos.

People from the north also migrated into the area. Sometimes they brought destruction to Byblos, but they also contributed to the culture.

Trade with Egypt again flourished between the twentieth and eighteenth centuries B.C. Byblos enjoyed a period of prestige, and the rulers of the city were the only ones in the East to whom the Egyptians referred with the title of prince.

In addition to Byblos, other city-states such as Acco and Tyre were independent, according to Egyptian texts. Although the Egyptians were the dominant power force in the area during the period, these city-states also traded with Syria and Mesopotamia and exchanged diplomatic envoys and gifts.

Then in the eighteenth century B.C. another group, the Hyksos, took control of Egypt and disrupted its relations with the city-states to the north. Not much is known about what happened to the area that is now Lebanon during the next two centuries, but at the end of that time, the political power structure of the area had changed. Egypt regained control of the coastal cities as far north as Ugarit (now in western Syria). However, two other kingdoms challenged the Egyptians in the Syrian area.

During this period the city-states were experimenting with a better way to communicate with others. Neither the hieroglyphics (pictorial writing) of the Egyptians nor the cuneiform (ancient wedge-shaped system of writing) of the Mesopotamians was satisfactory. Some of these early attempts to simplify the number of forms for writing foreshadowed the development of the alphabet that was completed, or at least transmitted, by the

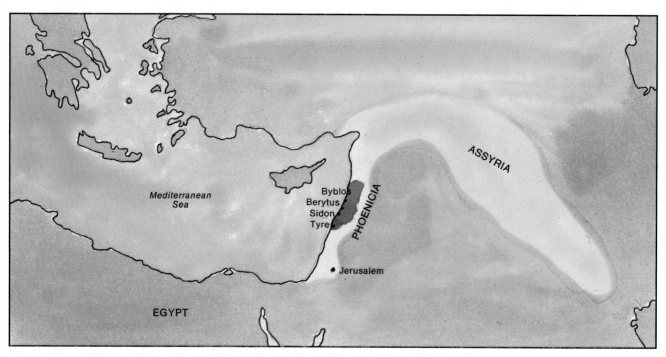

The eastern Mediterranean area about 1200 B.C. Lebanon of today is shown in orange.

Phoenicians in the thirteenth to twelfth centuries B.C. Also the religious life, the art forms, and the trade of this period show that the Phoenicians took much of the earlier culture into their civilization.

THE PHOENICIANS

Although there is no surviving literature and modern buildings stand over the ancient remains, historians do know about the Phoenicians' civilization. Neighboring countries wrote about the Phoenicians in records that *do* remain. The Old Testament is especially important because it comes from a close neighbor and was written while events were occurring. Mesopotamian and Egyptian sources also make mention of the Phoenicians. Greek and Roman historians provide information, too.

It was the Roman historian, Justin, who said that the inhabitants of Sidon, one of the early cities, founded Tyre. Since

*Ruins in Tyre from earlier
civilizations: Roman baths (above)
and a Crusader castle (left)*

Tyre had been established before 1200 B.C., the date assigned by
Justin, it may be that the people of Sidon settled in and gave the
town importance. Sidon seemed to be a very important city at this
period since in both the Old Testament and the poems of Homer
the word "Sidonians" is used to mean Phoenicians. The
Phoenicians also are sometimes called Canaanites.

The Phoenician kingdoms were fairly independent at this time
as is demonstrated by the story of an Egyptian representative who
had been sent to buy timber. Instead of showing him the same
respect that had been shown to the Egyptian *pharaohs* (rulers) in
the past, the Phoenician prince of Byblos let the Egyptian wait for
days before he talked with him. Then the prince stated that he was
not a servant to the Egyptian or his pharaoh. From such stories
and from various inscriptions that have been discovered, it
appears that Byblos had a series of kings, mostly related to each
other, from the mid-tenth to the early ninth century B.C.—a fact
indicating some stability and independence.

However, the Assyrian Empire (a group from northern Syria) was somewhat of a challenge to the Phoenicians. The first expedition to the area by the Assyrian king, Tiglath-pileser I, is thought to have occurred about 1100 B.C. This king boasted of tribute in the form of timber from the Lebanese mountains he received from the Phoenician cities of Byblos, Sidon, and Aradus. Tribute was an annual or specified sum of money or other valuable thing paid by one ruler or nation to another as the price of peace and protection.

During this time, the city of Tyre became increasingly important. King Hiram, who ruled from 969 to 936 B.C., had many foreign contacts. Both the Old Testament and Josephus, an ancient historian who said he was reporting from the *Annals of Tyre* (now lost), describe Hiram's relationship to Kings David and Solomon of Israel. The infamous Jezebel, who was married to King Ahab of Israel, was a princess of Tyre. The Tyrians eventually colonized along the coast of present-day Lebanon and into Africa. One of the kings of Tyre, Pygmalion, who reigned from 820 to 774 B.C., was in power when the Tyrians reached the North African coast and founded the city of Carthage—later the center of the Phoenician civilization and now called Tunis—in Tunisia. Carthage is said to have been established when the Tyrian princess, Elissa-Dido, fled to escape her brother, Pygmalion. Eventually, she killed herself to avoid being married to Iarbas, an African chief.

The ninth and early eighth centuries B.C. were a prosperous period for the Phoenicians. They apparently got along with the Assyrians and traded in the distant corners of their world. The Phoenicians had two kinds of ships. Transport ships had rounded hulls for cargo space (four times as long as their width), rectangular sails, and carried a crew usually of less than twenty.

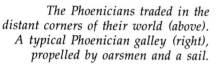

The Phoenicians traded in the distant corners of their world (above). A typical Phoenician galley (right), propelled by oarsmen and a sail.

Warships were narrower (seven times as long as the width) and carried a larger crew to man the oars and change the sails. While transport ships usually would take a route along the coastline, picking up and selling goods from ports along their routes, deep sea navigation was possible. The Ursa Minor constellation was used in navigation, and the ancient world called it the "Phoenician star." It also is called the Little Dipper.

Phoenician artistic products were much in demand in the royal courts of the world. Ivory inlaid furniture, carved gems, golden jewelry, glass, and especially purple cloth, were prized. The dye, made from molluscs found in the shallow waters of the Mediterranean, was an indelible purple. The color could range from dark red to violet. The Phoenicians controlled and kept secret the process for the manufacture of this dye, and it was so costly that only kings and rich nobles could afford garments dyed with it. That is how purple became a symbol of royalty. Glass,

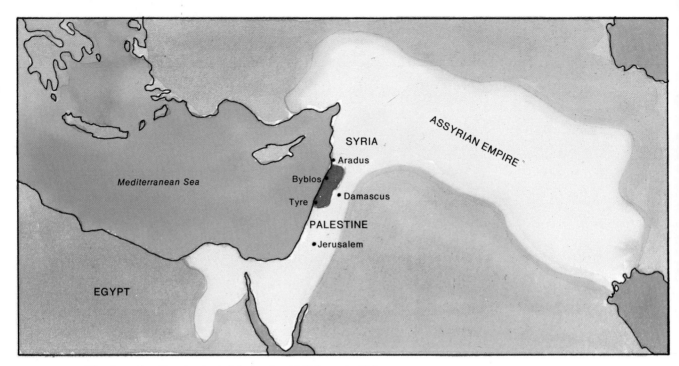

The Assyrian Empire lasted from about 1100 B.C. to 612 B.C.
Lebanon of today is shown in orange.

though not invented by the Phoenicians, was perfected with high-quality sand from the beaches. Small glass flasks and containers earned maximum profit and could be carried in a small space in the ships.

The Phoenician alphabet was adopted by neighbors, and the simplified writing was important for trade. The tribute that they paid to the Assyrians did not seem to restrict the Phoenicians' ability to prosper, with private merchants and shipowners taking over some of the power of the city kings.

However, the attitude of the Assyrian kings changed radically in the middle of the eighth century B.C. when the Assyrians conquered the Phoenician kings. When the city of Sidon dared to revolt, the Assyrian king Esarhaddon, who ruled from 681 to 668 B.C., said he meted out the following punishment: "I razed to the ground Sidon, the fortified city in the middle of the sea, destroyed and cast into the sea its walls and dwellings, annihilated the place

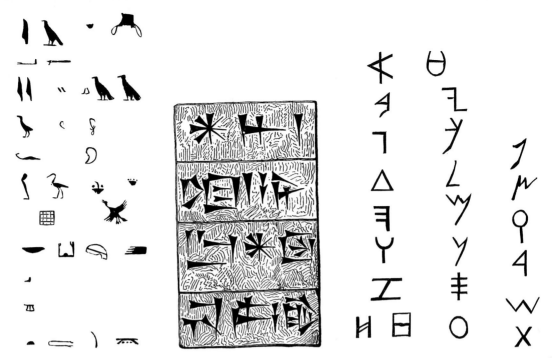

Egyptian hieroglyphics (left) and Mesopotamian cuneiform (center) eventually led to the alphabet used by the Phoenicians (right) in the thirteenth to twelfth centuries B.C.

where it stood. As to Abdi-milkutti, its king, who in the face of my armies had fled into the middle of the sea, I cut off his head. I deported his subjects, who were innumerable, to Assyria. I reordered the territory placing one of my officials to govern over them."

When Tyrians revolted, their king was made a servant and their commercial activities were restricted. A second revolt resulted in the Assyrian king brutally suppressing the people and having them sent to Assyria as slaves.

It is easy to imagine the satisfaction of the Phoenicians when the Assyrian Empire was overthrown by the Medes in 612 B.C. However, the Egyptian influence in the area at the end of the seventh century B.C. was strong. Herodotus, the Greek historian, reports that around the end of the seventh century B.C., the Phoenicians, on behalf of the Egyptian pharaoh Necho, sailed around Africa on a three-year journey.

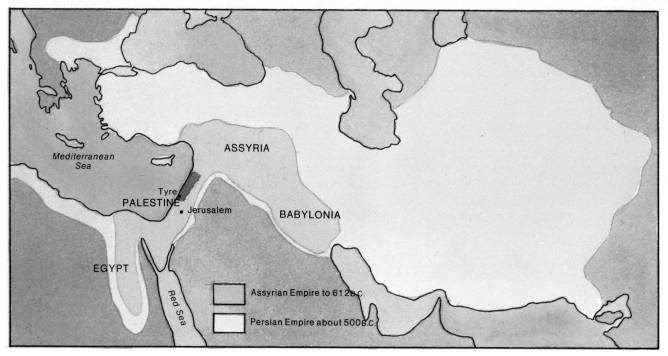

The Assyrian and Persian empires in the sixth and seventh centuries B.C.   Lebanon of today is shown in orange.

Eventually Babylonians (from present-day southern Iraq) defeated the Egyptians and the Babylonian king Nebuchadnezzar II ruled from 605 to 562 B.C. Tyre was able to hold out for thirteen more years, but eventually was conquered. The Babylonians frequently selected the local rulers. During one period between 564 and 556 B.C., Tyre had a republican form of government administered by judges.

When the Persian Empire (present-day Iran) conquered the Babylonians, the Phoenicians were treated well because of their strategic location as a military base for operations against Greece and Egypt. The Phoenician kings were given new territory and commanded the naval units of their cities personally. At first the Phoenicians were strongly pro-Persian in the fight against the Greeks. But as the Persian Empire broke down, more pro-Greek sentiment appeared.

Alexander the Great and his Greek army beat the Persians at the Battle of Issus in 333 B.C. Many of the Phoenicians viewed the

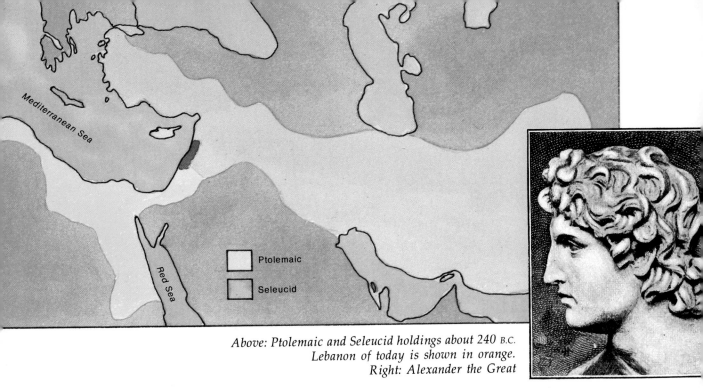

Above: Ptolemaic and Seleucid holdings about 240 B.C.
Lebanon of today is shown in orange.
Right: Alexander the Great

defeat as a liberation. Byblos and Sidon greeted the Greeks, but
Tyre held out. Alexander built a causeway (road) out to the island
stronghold of Tyre. It took months to construct, but then
Alexander's army was able to attack Tyre by land as well as by
sea. Two thousand male Tyrians were crucified along the shore of
the island, and thirty thousand women, children, and aged were
sold as slaves. While Tyre was under siege, Alexander led a
campaign against the Arabian tribes in the Anti-Lebanon
Mountains. The Greek Empire (also called Hellenistic or
Macedonian) swallowed up the Phoenician civilization in the area
that is now Lebanon. But Phoenician culture flourished in the
former colonies such as Carthage (now in Tunisia) and extended
across the western Mediterranean as far as Spain.

THE GREEKS

Alexander continued his conquest of territory to the east, all the
way into India. Phoenician traders and sailors joined Alexander's

35

campaigns. His early death in 323 B.C. resulted in fighting among his generals and a division of his empire. Ptolemy in Egypt, Seleucus in Babylonia, Antigonus in Asia Minor (part of present-day Turkey), and Antipater in Macedonia (part of the Greek Empire then) took power. The cities of Phoenicia were fought over, won, and lost by many different generals, with the chief powers being the Seleucids in the north and the Ptolemies in the south. The cities were Ptolemaic from 286 to 198 B.C. and Seleucid from 198 to 182 B.C. Hellenistic culture was predominant in both camps with the religion, festivals, and the gymnastic contests of the Greeks being observed. As Seleucid power waned, the Phoenician cities gained some measure of independence, but the period was one of conflict.

During the Hellenistic period trade was revived. Luxuries from the East and slave trade based on prisoners of war and kidnapped victims of piracy flourished. Agricultural production of new items such as pistachio nuts from Persia together with the old standbys of wine from grapes and oil from olives increased. Purple-dyed cloth and glass were still popular. Iron and copper mines were worked. Papyrus rolls were replacing clay tablets as writing materials. Papyrus was made from the stem of the papyrus plant. "Bible" is the Greek word for papyrus, named after the Phoenician city of Byblos, from which papyrus was exported.

Greek philosophy and literature were now part of the education of the well-to-do. While the Canaanite language, which was spoken by the Phoenicians, remained that of every day, Greek was used for scholarly purposes. Gradually, the Aramaic language began to be used. The Greeks picked up some of the local gods and identified them with their own gods.

It is difficult to identify Greek literature that may have been

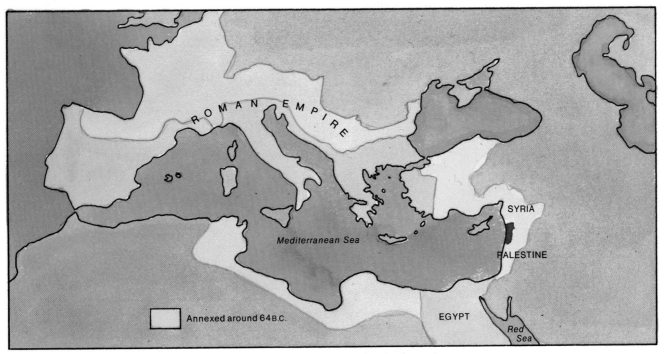

Roman Empire around 64 B.C. Lebanon of today is shown in orange.

written by Phoenician writers using Greek pen names; it is easier
to determine philosophers with Phoenician backgrounds. Zeno,
the founder of the Stoic school of philosophy, was born in the
Phoenician colony of Cyprus (on the present-day island of
Cyprus). His system of philosophy taught that the only good is
virtue and the only evil is moral weakness. Under this
philosophy, the wise man has what is good regardless of his other
problems. Other Phoenician philosophers were Boethus of Sidon,
who studied astronomy; Antipater of Tyre; Diodorus; and
another Zeno of Sidon who studied geometry.

THE ROMANS

The Romans under the general Pompey took over the territory
of Phoenicia in 64 B.C. Pompey incorporated the territory of
Phoenicia, Palestine, and Syria in one Roman province called

A bridge and aqueduct near Beirut built by the Romans.

Provincia Syria. The leading cities at that time—Tyre, Sidon, Tripoli, and Aradus—were granted rights of self-government. The Roman ruler Julius Caesar gave privileges to some of the former Phoenician cities. Roman general Marc Antony gave the Egyptian Queen Cleopatra the Bekaa Valley and some of the coastal cities down toward Egypt.

The coming of the Roman Empire and Christianity into the territory changed life for the people. The Romans brought some political stability; they also built roads, bridges, harbors, canals, and cisterns (reservoirs). They were successful in limiting the operations of pirates and robbers. The population expanded inland, not only to the cooler mountain areas but also to the valley where, at Heliopolis (present-day Baalbek), a huge temple complex was built around A.D. 138 to 217. At the site of ancient shrines, large buildings were erected for the worship of the Roman gods Jupiter and Bacchus.

The Phoenician language was now replaced by Aramaic for the natives of the area and Latin, the Roman language, for the officials. Trade flourished, and glass vases signed by Ennion of Sidon in the first century A.D. have been found in Egypt, Cyprus, Italy, and southern Russia. Cedar wood was still prized, but the Roman Emperor Hadrian put up boundary markers to preserve some of the forests.

Emperor Septimus Serverus married Julia Domna from the province of present-day Lebanon, beginning the dynasty of Syrian-Lebanese emperors of Rome from A.D. 193 to 235. It was during this time that the Lebanese again migrated and settled throughout the empire in pursuit of their business interests. Even a few generations before this influx, a Roman writer, Juvenal, complained that the people of the Lebanese province had settled in Rome bringing their language, their customs, and their flutes and harps. They built places of worship dedicated to the gods of their territory just as modern immigrants from Lebanon have churches with altars dedicated to Our Lady of Lebanon.

The intellectual life of the Lebanese province was noted for famous philosophers, astronomers, mathematicians, and poets. Philo of Byblos wrote of the Phoenician religion. In the second century, Marinus of Tyre constructed maps using latitude and longitude and founded the mathematical geography on which Ptolemy, the famous astronomer and geographer from Egypt, based his work. Porphyry, born in Tyre in A.D. 223, went to Rome and collected the essays of his teacher, Plotinus, and published them. He wrote a famous essay against the Christians.

This area that is now Lebanon played a leading role in early Christianity. The New Testament describes Jesus' journey into the area near Tyre and Sidon and his healing of the daughter of a woman from that region (Matthew 15:22-28; Mark 7:24-31). People from these areas also went to hear Jesus teach and to be healed (Mark 3:8; Luke 6:17). When the apostles were first persecuted by those who opposed the new religion, they scattered to preach among other places in Phoenicia (Acts 11:19). The apostle Paul found a church in Tyre where he stayed for a week on one of his journeys and another in Sidon, a community where he stopped on his way to Rome (Acts 21:4-6; Acts 27:3). These towns were on routes that ran between Jerusalem and cities to the north.

Many students from various backgrounds were attracted to the schools of Berytus (now Beirut). The law school was famous. Two Roman jurists who were professors there were Papinian and Ulpian. Both were counselors to the emperors and had their writing incorporated in the law code, the *Digest*, of Justinian the Great. Outstanding Christian leaders such as Gregory, Thaumaturgus, Gregory Nazianzen, and Severus trained in Berytus.

The Romans persecuted the Christians because they would not worship the emperor as a god. It was not uncommon in the ancient world for a ruler to be given the worship due a god. At first, the Romans were comparatively mild in their actions against the Christians, and the Syrian-Lebanese emperors were rather tolerant. The last of that dynasty, Alexander Severus, refused to be worshiped as a god and had busts of Zoroaster, Abraham, and Jesus in his palace. However, in the great persecution from 303 to 313—during the reigns of Diocletian and Maximilian—churches were torn down and books were burned. Christians were dismissed from civil and military positions, and every Christian had to choose between allegiance and sacrifice to the gods of Rome or death.

Shortly thereafter, Christianity became the religion of the

Emperor Constantine founded Byzantium (now Istanbul, Turkey), the center of the Byzantine Empire.

kingdom under Emperor Constantine, who in 312 saw a vision of the cross in the sky. Constantine founded the capital that was to be the center of the Byzantine Empire, Byzantium (later Constantinople, and now Istanbul in Turkey).

The Roman Empire split in 395 when Emperor Theodosius the Great died leaving two sons—one to rule the West from Rome and the other to rule the Eastern empire from Byzantium. An earthquake in Berytus in 349 hastened the conversion to Christianity of persons who interpreted this disaster as a sign of God's wrath for some of the sexual practices in the temples of the local gods and goddesses. Other bad earthquakes and tidal waves hit Berytus, Tyre, Sidon, and Baalbek during the next two centuries and caused great damage to these cities. A quake and tidal wave in 552 and a fire in 560, which destroyed much of Berytus and killed thirty thousand persons, was a tragedy mourned in literature from Greece to Spain.

Wars with empires to the east, abuses and corruption in the running of the Byzantine Empire, heavy taxation on the people, and religious councils that could not resolve issues of faith to the satisfaction of all, resulted in a weakened government that was to be challenged by Arabs recently converted to Islam.

Chapter 4

FROM ARAB CONQUEST
TO INDEPENDENCE

Again the territory of present-day Lebanon was on the path of conquering forces. Arabs, Islamic dynasties, Crusaders from the West, Ottomans from Turkey, and the French under the World War I Allied Mandate—all found this territory had an important role in power politics.

ARAB CONQUEST AND THE UMAYYADS

The Islamic faith, based on the revelations to Muhammad in Arabia, inspired the next conquerors to come into the land. Under their new faith, Islam, the Muslims were no longer supposed to fight each other. They wanted to spread their faith and win new territory. Muslims were guaranteed a splendid afterlife if they should die in battle for their faith. Under the successor to Muhammad, Abu Bakr, the Muslims came out of Arabia and challenged the Byzantine Empire.

Led by General Khalid ibn al-Walid, they won in 636 against a larger army, made up mostly of mercenaries (persons fighting for pay), at the Battle of Yarmuk in what is now northwestern Jordan. In an earlier fight this general had marched for eighteen days across the Syrian desert with some eight hundred troops, with horses and camels. At Yarmuk he outmaneuvered his opponents and decisively defeated them.

The next *caliph* (ruler), Umar, then appointed Muawiyah, an Arab, to be governor of the territory that today includes Syria and Lebanon. Muawiyah was the founder of the Umayyad Dynasty that ruled from Damascus. He became caliph in 660. Persons adopting the faith of Islam were given the same rights and duties the conquerors had. Others were required to pay a toll and land tax.

The Muslim troops carried on further conquests in Mesopotamia and Persia to the northeast and to the southwest in Egypt and North Africa. The forests of Lebanon were again tapped for the first Muslim fleet, which was manned by the Lebanese who had been sailors since early Phoenician times. In a naval battle in 655, the Muslim fleet almost wiped out the Byzantine navy. The eastern Mediterranean area came under the control of the Arabs and the Lebanese coast was made relatively secure.

The history of the first four-and-a-half centuries under Islamic rule in the territory of present-day Lebanon is not well known because the Byzantine historians no longer focused on this land and the Arab historians were not yet concerned with it. During the time the Umayyads were in power, several groups of Christians sought refuge in the Lebanese mountains from persecution by the Byzantine emperor or the Muslim caliph. However, for the most part, the Umayyad caliphs were tolerant in religious and intellectual matters. Other ethnic groups and Muslim dissidents also found Lebanon a place of refuge.

THE ABBASIDS

The Umayyad Dynasty came to an end because of internal weaknesses and forces led by Abu al Abbas Abdullah, the great-great-grandson of Muhammad's uncle. After a nine-day battle in 750 in what is now Iraq, the Umayyads were defeated. The Lebanese cities surrendered peacefully. The rest of the Umayyad family was wiped out when some eighty princes were invited by Abdullah to a banquet near Jaffa (in present-day Israel) and then killed while they were at the feast.

The Abbasids established their capital at Baghdad (in Iraq) which, at the height of their power, was the center of intellectual achievements in philosophy, medicine, astronomy, and mathematics. Lebanon contributed several native sons to this culture: Rashid al-Din, a physician; al-Awazi, a lawyer and jurist; and Qusta ibn Luqa, a philosopher, physician, astronomer, and mathematician.

At first, the Abbasids treated Lebanon and neighboring countries as conquered territories. The harsh repression caused difficult relations between the new rulers and the residents. In protest against taxations, the Christians in the mountains revolted and seized several villages before they were stopped.

In 878, a deputy governor of Egypt took control of Palestine and parts of Syria, proclaiming independence from the Abbasids. Lebanon was cut off from Baghdad, the Abbasid capital, and came under the power of Egypt, as it had been in ancient times. After power changed hands several more times, the Fatimid Caliphate arose in Egypt with its founder claiming descent from Fatima, the daughter of the Prophet Muhammad. This new empire reached from the Atlantic Ocean to the Red Sea.

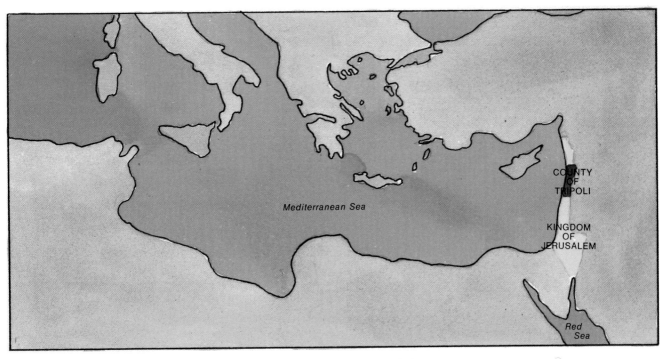

The eastern Mediterranean area around the time of the Crusades   Lebanon of today is shown in orange.

During this time the Byzantine army made several invasions into the territory that is now Lebanon without lasting success. The Turks also pushed into the area. Towns had local rulers who, while dependent on Egypt, tried to get along with powerful forces to the north. Still the territory seemed to prosper, and the visitors at that time were impressed with the supply of food and the cleanliness of the towns.

THE CRUSADES

The occupation and destruction by the Muslims of some of the holy places associated with the life of Jesus outraged some Christians. Pope Urban II in 1095 called on the Christians to recover these sites. With religious, economic, and political motivations, the leaders of Western Europe responded with eight

This engraving shows the Crusaders retreating from Lebanon (left) after their defeat by Saladin (above).

campaigns, known as the Crusades, which lasted from 1096 to 1291. After conquering Jerusalem, the Crusaders took Tripoli, Beirut, Sidon, and after a long siege, Tyre, to secure their lines of reinforcement by the sea. A Muslim general, Saladin, recaptured Jerusalem in 1187. The Crusaders lost ground after that and retreated from Lebanon.

The Muslims won a great victory, forcing the West out of the territory the Crusaders had claimed. Although the West was defeated, the Crusaders left behind castle forts whose ruins now dot the countryside. During this time the Christian Maronites in the territory acknowledged the pope and became open to Western influence. Moreover, the West took back to Europe new learning from the more civilized East and new products including paper and crops. Since then some Arabs are suspicious of people from the West, and that distrust influences world politics even today.

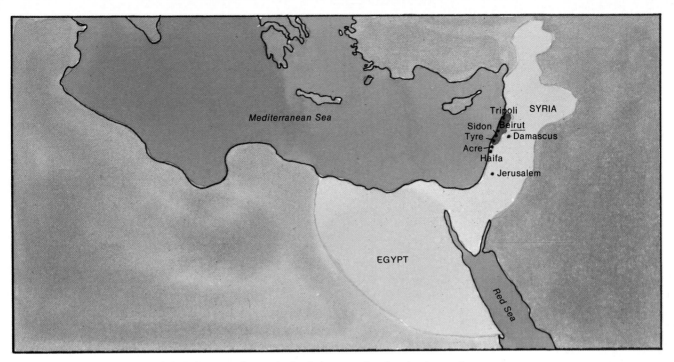

Mamluk Sultanate about 1350   Lebanon of today is shown in orange.

THE MAMLUKS

The thirteenth century was one of conflict in the territory that is now Lebanon, with Crusaders, the Mongols from the plains of Central Asia, and the Mamluks from Egypt fighting for the land. The Mamluks, who won, were originally slaves from the area east of the Caspian Sea and from the mountains between the Black Sea and the Caspian Sea. They were imported by the *sultans* (rulers) in Egypt to serve as their bodyguards. However, in the thirteenth century one of the slaves killed the Egyptian sultan and started a Mamluk Dynasty that ruled Egypt and Syria for two centuries.

This period was one in which there was a crackdown against the local Christians and Jews as well as the Muslim sects other than the Sunnis. Many of the local governors were tyrannical and incompetent. Moreover, the population suffered famine, drought, earthquake, and the plague. In nearby Damascus, the Black Death of 1348 was said to have killed two thousand citizens per day in

47

its final stages. It is estimated that under the Mamluks the entire population was reduced about one-third.

Despite the harsh conditions, the Lebanese land tenants had certain rights that were denied to those in Syria and Egypt. They could change location and choose the landholder for whom to work. Moreover, contacts with the West were reestablished, and Beirut became a trading center. Tripoli became a center of government where four mosque schools were established. Also, learning was preserved by *sufis* (Islamic mystics), dervish fraternities (dervishes were famed for whirling or dancing to cause a trance), hospitals that engaged in medical teaching, and Christian monasteries where manuscripts were copied, preserved, and transmitted.

Two new powers arose to threaten the Mamluks: The Ottomans from Turkey and the Safawids in Persia. The Mamluks allied themselves with the Safawids because the Safawids were viewed as less of a threat. The Ottomans used artillery, muskets, and long-range weapons against the Mamluk forces, who did not have such military equipment. The Ottomans easily won a complete victory in Syria in 1516. The area peacefully became Ottoman territory for the next four centuries, and the Ottomans went on to subdue Egypt.

During their rule the Mamluks had succeeded in turning the land that was to be Lebanon away from European (especially French) influence and back to the East.

THE OTTOMANS

Under the Ottomans, the conquered people (especially the ones who were not Muslims) were allowed to live in their own fashion

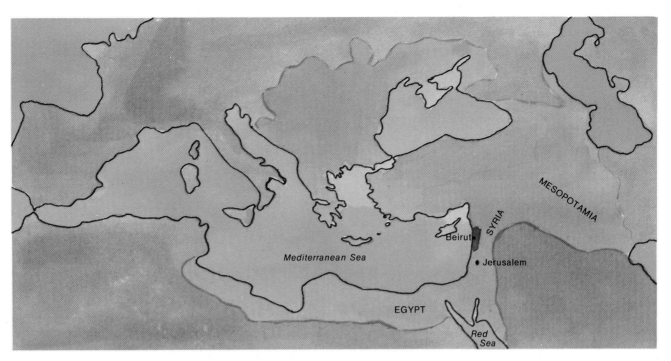

The Ottoman Empire from 1529 to 1789
Lebanon of today is shown in orange.

as long as they gave no trouble and supplied the needs of the conquerors. The Ottomans differed from the Arabs. The Ottomans maintained a class of governors, political advisors, and generals and admirals over whom the sultan had the power of life and death. They differed from the Arabs in dividing the executive duties of government that the sultan controlled from the administration of the law—both the Islamic religious law that was delegated to persons called *ulema* and the civil law that developed later into lay courts.

Also the Ottomans classified people according to their religious beliefs. Under this system all non-Muslim groups had their own religious leaders who administered family and estate law and supervised religious education and organization. Thus, for example, all Greek Orthodox were lumped together regardless of the language or country of origin of the believers. Further complicating this attempt to deal with minorities was the practice

49

of identifying these religious groups with other nations. The Maronites and other Catholics were aligned with France, the Greek Orthodox with Russia, and the Protestants with Great Britain.

In the war with the Mamluks, the local rulers, called *emirs*, "princes," had allied themselves with the winning side. The Ottoman sultan, impressed with the eloquence of the ruler Emir Fakhr al-Din I, granted the Lebanese rulers a semiautonomous status. The Ottomans ruled through two important feudal Lebanese families, the Maans and the Shihabs, until the middle of the nineteenth century.

The Maan family had come to Lebanon in 1120 to defend the country against the Crusaders. They settled on the southwestern part of the Lebanon mountains and accepted the Druze beliefs.

When the last leader from the Maan family died in 1697 without an heir apparent, the Shihab family from southern Lebanon succeeded to power. Bashir II was the most famous of this family. In power when Napoleon laid siege to Acre in present-day Israel, Bashir remained neutral. Napoleon gave up and returned to Egypt. Later in an attempt to break away from the Ottomans, Bashir allied himself with Mohammad Ali, the founder of modern Egypt.

The Egyptian troops, with those of Bashir II, occupied Damascus, Syria. Other religious groups and European powers entered the affairs until some European powers signed the London Treaty with the Ottoman Turks in 1840 calling on Egypt to get out of Syria. When confronted with Ottoman and British troops, the Egyptians left and Bashir II surrendered to the British and went into exile.

Under Bashir III, the Christians and the Druze engaged in bitter fights. A number of other ideas were tried, including the suggestion of some of the European nations that the country be divided between the Christians and the Druze. With the French supporting the Christians, the British supporting the Druze, and the Ottomans trying to abolish the semiautonomous status of the country, things went from bad to worse.

One of the peasant leaders, Tanyos Shahlin, demanded in 1858 that the feudal (landowning) class should have no special privileges. When the demand was refused, the peasants burned the homes of the sheikhs who lived on Mount Lebanon. In 1860 the Druze massacred some of the Maronites. The French tried to intervene. The Turkish government sent the minister of foreign affairs to Beirut and informed the French that measures had been taken against the leaders of the massacres. An international commission formed in 1860 by France, Great Britain, Russia, Austria, Prussia, and Turkey investigated the causes of the conflict and proposed new measures to prevent repetition of the fighting.

The commission decided that the partition of Lebanon in 1842 had set off the religious wars. It was recommended that the country be reunited under a Christian *mutassarif*, "governor," to be appointed by the Turkish sultan. The mutassarif was to be assisted by an administrative council composed of twelve members chosen from the different religious communities in the territory. The first mutassarif was opposed by the Maronite leader, Yussif Karam, because the new governor was an Armenian and not a Lebanese. Karam went into exile in Italy, but on his death his body was returned to his village southeast of Tripoli where he is remembered today as a nationalist leader.

During this period, many Lebanese who were restricted to the mountains under the new arrangement decided to emigrate to

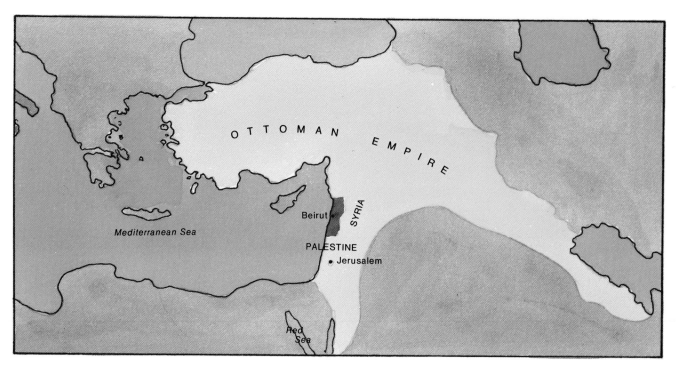

Above: The Ottoman Empire in 1914   Lebanon of today is shown in orange.
Below: The American University of Beirut

other countries. They went to Egypt, other parts of Africa, North and South America, and even the Far East. They took with them their customs and their religion. They sent money back home to their families and sometimes returned to Lebanon after making their fortunes.

Also during this period, foreign missionaries established schools. The American University of Beirut was founded in 1866, and the French Saint Joseph's University was established in Beirut in 1875. The new intellectual circle gave birth to new Arabic literature. Publications and newspapers were started during this era. A new sense of Arab identity, supported by both Christians and Muslims, and dissatisfaction with the harsh Turkish rule resulted in secret political groups and parties wanting the same rights for Arabs that the Turks had.

WORLD WAR I

Turkey entered World War I in 1914 on the side of the Central Powers and ended Lebanon's semiautonomous status, replacing the mutassarif with a Turk. The Turkish general, Jamal Pasha, was unsuccessful in an attack against the British defending the Suez Canal. He executed hundreds of Christians and Muslims and he established a blockade around Lebanon. Famine and plague wiped out more of the population. The Turkish army cut down trees for fuel for trains and military purposes. Lebanon suffered perhaps more than any of the other Ottoman territories.

In 1918 the British General Edmund Allenby and Faisal I, who would be king of the soon-to-be-formed country of Iraq, marched

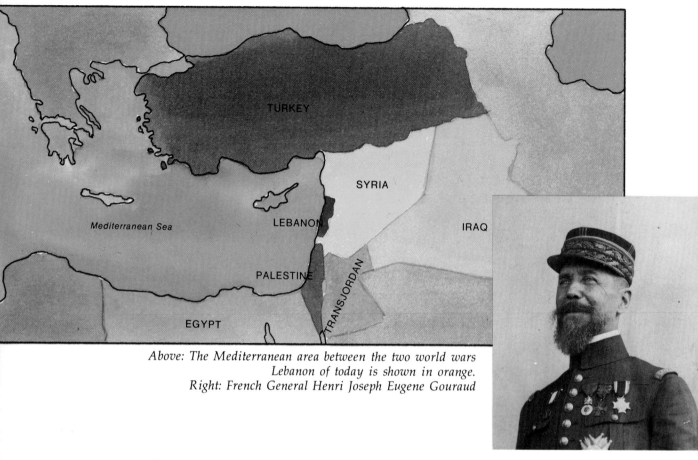

*Above: The Mediterranean area between the two world wars
Lebanon of today is shown in orange.
Right: French General Henri Joseph Eugene Gouraud*

into Palestine, and Allied forces were able to occupy Syria and
Lebanon. At the San Remo Conference at the conclusion of World
War I, in April 1920, Lebanon and Syria were placed under the
French Mandate and General Henri Gouraud.

THE MANDATE

On September 1, 1940, General Gouraud proclaimed the
establishment of Greater Lebanon with Beirut as its capital.
Charles Debbas was elected the first president under the French
Mandate. At the end of Debbas's second term, two candidates
sought the office. The Chamber of Deputies was divided in their

support of the two and some proposed the name of a third—a Muslim leader of Tripoli. The French high commissioner, Henri Ponsot, suspended the constitution rather than see a Muslim elected. Ponsot extended the term of Debbas for a year. The French did not approve of this tactic. They recalled Ponsot and appointed Comte Damien de Martel as high commisioner. Then, Emile Edde was elected president by the Chamber of Deputies. Edde partially restored the constitution, but with the outbreak of World War II in September 1939, the high commissioner again suspended the constitution.

France was occupied by the Germans in 1940. The Vichy Government (named after the city where the German-controlled French government ruled) installed by the Germans in France appointed General Dentz as high commissioner. Edde resigned as president of Greater Lebanon, and Alfred Naccash was appointed by the Vichy forces. When the Franco-British troops advanced into Lebanon, Vichy control was ended. An armistice was signed in Acre on July 14, 1941.

During the period of the mandate, the French had tried to rebuild and strengthen the Lebanese economy. They repaired and enlarged the Beirut harbor and built roads linking the major cities. They developed new administrative and judicial systems and a new code of laws governing civil procedure. They put efforts into improving the educational system, agriculture, public health, and living conditions.

As a result of pressure from the Lebanese and from the international community, General Georges Catroux acting for French General Charles de Gaulle proclaimed Lebanon independent on November 26, 1941.

Chapter 5

YEARS OF CONFLICT

At last the Lebanese had a formal declaration of independence. The years after World War II brought economic prosperity, with the wealthy seeking out Beirut as a resort on the Mediterranean, and also great conflict. Lebanon became the battlefield on which internal forces and foreign powers killed combatants and civilians alike.

FRENCH CONTROL

In spite of their proclamation of independence for Lebanon, the French needed encouragement to relinquish control. On November 11, 1943, the French arrested the president and most of the high government officials. Revolt by the people and intervention by the British forced the French to restore the government and transfer administrative power to the Lebanese. By 1946 Lebanon was independent, with no foreign troops on its soil, and had become a member of the United Nations and the Arab League.

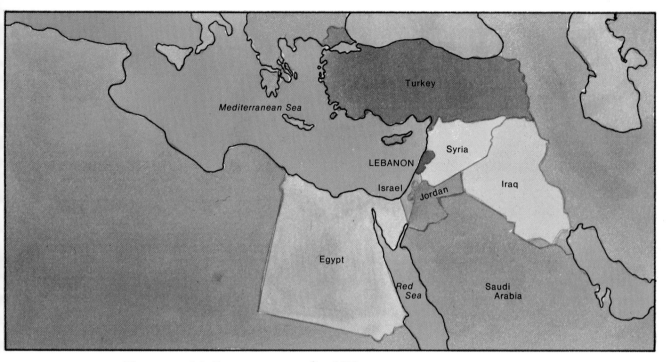

The eastern Mediterranean area after 1950

THE KHURI PRESIDENCY

Bishara al-Khuri, a Maronite, was elected president and worked closely with Riad as-Sulh, a Sunni, who was premier for most of Khuri's term. There were economic problems following World War II. Foreign spending in Lebanon decreased. War shortages in Europe that had initially favored Lebanese trade were disappearing. The devaluation of the French franc, to which the Lebanese currency had been tied, hurt the economy. Lebanon's refusal to enter into a full economic and financial union with Syria brought sanctions and disruption of trade with Syria. All these factors produced a high cost of living and a great deal of unemployment by 1952.

Smoke rises from the old walled city of Jerusalem during the fighting between the Arabs and the Israelis in 1948 (left). Palestinians who fled into Lebanon were housed on the outskirts of Beirut (right).

Across Lebanon's southern border, when the British ended their mandate and withdrew their forces in 1948, Israel declared itself an independent Jewish state. The Arab states—Lebanon, Syria, Jordan, Egypt, and Iraq—refused to accept Israel's existence and declared war on the Jewish state. Some Palestinians living in Israel fled across the border into Lebanon and other neighboring states as a result of fighting between the Israelis and the Palestinians. In 1949 Lebanon, Egypt, Jordan, and Syria each signed an armistice agreement with Israel mediated by the United Nations.

In Lebanon, an attempt by the Syrian Socialist Nationalist party to overthrow the government by force was put down, and their leader was executed. The party retaliated by assassinating the premier. Increasing opposition to Khuri was expressed in a general strike that forced his resignation in 1952.

Camille Chamoun served as president of Lebanon from 1952 to 1958.

THE CHAMOUN PRESIDENCY

After Khuri, Camille Chamoun was elected by Parliament in 1952 to succeed to the presidency. Amir Khalid Chebab was the prime minister. Certain constitutional reforms were undertaken such as granting the vote to women, revision of the press laws, and reorganization of the judicial system. While still trying to maintain a balance among the various religious interests, the electoral districts were increased with the hope that a more national perspective rather than a tribal one would result.

While discussion of economic issues with Syria did not appear to be productive, the government had more success with encouraging internal development. In 1955, for example, the World Bank granted Lebanon a loan of $27 million for the Litani River project that was to double the available electric power and provide irrigation of a large area along the coast.

Developments in neighboring countries continued their effect in Lebanon. During the Suez Crisis of 1956, Lebanon refused to break off diplomatic relations with France and Britain, who had conspired and fought with Israel in the war against Egypt where the Suez Canal was located. Lebanon also took advantage of the Eisenhower Doctrine under which the United States offered financial, economic, and military aid to the Middle East countries. Lebanon received $20 million in assistance. These two events, in particular, caused other Middle East countries to see Lebanon as being too pro-Western.

TENSIONS INCREASE

As the 1957 elections drew close, rioting erupted and was put down with the aid of troops. There was opposition to the pro-Western policies, and after a siege of bombings and assassinations, the government imposed a close control over all Palestinian refugees in the country. After further violence, the northern area of Lebanon was declared a military sector.

In 1958 Lebanon announced that it refused to join either the union with Syria and Egypt—called the United Arab Republic (UAR)—or the union with Iraq and Jordan—called the Arab Federation. Lebanon chose to remain independent. The UAR wanted the return of the predominantly Arab sectors that had been joined to Lebanon at the time of the French Mandate. The pro-Arab sections in the north, in Beirut, and in the south caused serious disturbances. United States information centers in Beirut and Tripoli were destroyed, and Lebanon asked the United States for support.

The United States sent arms and police equipment and reinforced its Sixth Fleet that was stationed in the Mediterranean. The Soviet Union accused the United States of interference.

United States troops arriving in Lebanon in 1958

Lebanon appealed to the Arab League to stop the interference of the UAR in its internal affairs. Since the Arab League was unable to decide on action to be taken, Lebanon appealed to the United Nations, who sent in observers.

When a coup upset the government in Iraq, President Chamoun asked for American troops to maintain the security and independence of Lebanon. The United States sent in marines with the understanding that they would be withdrawn if requested by Lebanon or if the United Nations took measures to provide protection. The United Nations adopted a measure that provided for the evacuation of the American troops under the auspices of the UN and the Arab League.

THE CHEHAB AND HELOU REGIMES

General Fouad Chehab, who had acted with restraint in the 1958 crisis, was elected president. He invited the leader of the Tripoli insurgents to be prime minister and worked in other ways to gain the support of the Muslims.

*In 1964 Charles Helou (left) became president and in 1970
Sulayman Franjiya (right) was sworn in as president.*

The country was strong economically because of capital
invested from less stable Arab countries. On December 31, 1961,
there was one unsuccessful attempt to overthrow the government
by military and civilians identified with a group that wanted to
join Arab countries in a new Greater Syria. The president was
urged to seek another term, but he refused.

In 1964 Charles Helou was elected president. A financial crisis
in 1966 resulted from massive withdrawals from one of the
Lebanese banks and the expansion of the banking system based on
the oil money from Saudi Arabia and the Gulf states. Among the
problems was the increasing number and intensity of the clashes
between the Israelis and Palestinian forces. In the 1967 "Six-Day"
War, Israel gained control of more land forcing more Palestinians
to flee.

Lebanon was drawn into the fight of the Palestinians and the
Arab States against Israel. At the end of 1968, in reprisal for an
attack against an Israeli airliner at the Athens airport, Israeli
commandos raided the Beirut airport and destroyed thirteen
planes belonging to the Lebanese. The United Nations Security
Council unanimously voted to condemn Israel for this raid.

By late summer 1969, Palestinian fighters developed new bases for attacks on Israel. Their raids on Israel and the reprisals by the Israelis caused conflict with the regular Lebanese army. The army was reported to have attacked Palestinian forces in some of the refugee camps; however, the government disclaimed authorizing the army's action. Palestinian fighters took over Tripoli for several days, and the refugee camps were turned into training and equipping centers for them. There were threats of military intervention by Syria and Iraq to support the Palestinians.

In November the leader of the Lebanese army and Yasser Arafat, head of al-Fatah (a component of the Palestine Liberation Organization—PLO), signed a cease-fire agreement in Cairo that set limits on Palestinian operations in and around Lebanon. These measures were to protect the Lebanese and their property from the retaliation of the Israelis.

In May the Israelis mounted a major air and ground attack on the Palestinian forces in southern Lebanon and occupied a great deal of territory for two days. Syria supplied air support to the Lebanese forces.

THE FRANJIYA PRESIDENCY

In August 1970, Sulayman Franjiya was elected president. Strikes, demonstrations, and fighting marked the years between 1970 and 1974. Unemployment and inflation followed the move of people from the rural areas into cities. Some 40 percent of the population of the country had moved into Beirut, forming enclaves based on ethnic and religious lines. By 1973 one in every ten persons in Lebanon was a Palestinian. They were poor and landless. They identified with the more radical rural poor groups in Lebanon. Tensions increased as the Israeli commandos attacked bases and camps and even killed opposition leaders in their Beirut homes. Various political groups in Lebanon, including the right-wing Christian Phalangist group composed of Maronite Christians, began training their own militia; and the danger of action by private armies increased.

Lebanon did not enter the Arab-Israeli Wars of 1967 and 1973. Other Arab countries questioned Lebanon's loyalty. There were rumors of secret agreements with Israel. Border fighting in southern Lebanon continued between the Israelis and the Palestinian forces. The skirmishes resulted in death, injury, and property damage not only for the Palestinian fighters but also for the Lebanese residents. The government was unable to curb the fighting, and the Phalangists fought the Palestinians with much damage in Beirut.

THE CIVIL WAR

In April 1975 Palestinian fighters attacked some Christian Phalangists. In response the Phalangists killed Palestinian passengers on a bus. This triggered fighting between the Christians and Muslims. The fighting spread and continued, with only brief interruptions, until October 1976. While the official policy of both the PLO and the Lebanese army was not to intervene, breakaway groups from both sides became involved in the fighting. Foreign countries backed different groups. Muslims began winning to such an extent that it appeared that Lebanon would either be divided or become a left-wing Arab state. Syria, believing that such a result would force an Israeli attack, shifted support to the Christians.

The Israelis blockaded the ports of Tyre and Sidon and invaded territory in southern Lebanon. Some Lebanese, backed by Iraq and Libya, began courting the PLO, which they had previously claimed to be ineffective. Egypt also sought closer relations with the PLO to support political moves that it had taken. The Christians, who were aided by Syrian tanks and troops, began to win the war.

In an attempt to separate the fighting groups, the country was divided along a "Green Line" that passed through the center of Beirut along a road to Damascus. The Christians were in the north, with a leftist Druze-Muslim-Palestinian government to the south. Attempts to end the fighting were initially unsuccessful. In November 1976 an Arab League peacekeeping force of thirty thousand troops (mostly Syrian) under the direction of the newly installed President Elias Sarkis and the command of a Lebanese Sunni officer brought the civil war to an end, although sporadic fighting continues.

The war left Lebanon badly damaged. The fighting had created such bitterness that a resolution of the governmental problem seemed impossible. The Muslims were the majority, but the Christians were determined to keep control of key government positions. This would protect the Christians from the second-class status of minorities they had in some of the neighboring Muslim countries. The Palestinians had suffered the death of perhaps twenty thousand persons with twice that number wounded. They also had lost their bid for power. The Lebanese Christians now had even more reason to be in the debt of Israel. Arabs in all countries began to question the dream of pan-Arabism—a unity for all Arabs—because Arabs did not present a unified front in world politics.

Armed Muslims take over a Lebanese army tank (left) during the civil war. After the cease-fire, people view the rubble (top). In November 1976 Elias Sarkis (above) became president.

Chapter 6

YEARS OF CHAOS

Inside Lebanon in 1976, factions were armed for combat. With Israel on its border, and Middle East nations engaging in a power struggle for influence in the country, Lebanon faced more years of chaos.

ISRAELI INVASION AND WITHDRAWAL

The government under President Sarkis set up a Cabinet of "technocrats" charged with reconstruction of the country. Localized fighting followed by cease-fires was sporadic through 1978. An Israeli retaliation in southern Lebanon in March 1978 led to a United Nations Interim Force (UNIFIL) to keep the peace when the Israelis withdrew a few months later. Fighting between the Syrian troops and the Christian militias was the cause for the meeting of eight foreign ministers of Arab countries at Beiteddin, near Beirut, in 1978. In the Beiteddin Declaration, the foreign ministers called for a Lebanese central authority with a truly national army and limitations on the armed militias of the various groups.

Instead, fighting continued with a right-wing Lebanese army officer proclaiming an independent free Lebanon in 695 square

Israeli army tanks travel through Sidon on the way to Beirut in 1982.

miles (1,800 square kilometers) next to the Israeli border. Syrian, Christian, and Israeli forces challenged one another, but a special United States Middle East envoy, Philip Habib, was able to work out a cease-fire effective in July 1981. Because of the conflict, it was hard for the government to carry on regular activity and get sufficient agreement on projects to make them work.

On July 17, 1981, the Israelis bombed the PLO headquarters in Beirut. The PLO continued to attack Israel from Syrian-occupied Lebanon. In June 1982, Israel invaded Lebanon with an estimated sixty thousand troops. The Israelis pursued the retreating Syrian army up the Bekaa Valley and led attacks on the coastal towns. The fighting continued, with Syria refusing to leave until the Israelis did. The government controlled only a small part of the central section of the country.

The United States tried to negotiate another cease-fire. An agreement was signed in May 1983 by Lebanon and Israel under which Israel would withdraw its forces. However, Israel indicated that it would do so only if Syria would withdraw from the Bekaa

Photographs taken in 1982 show the damage that was done to a business area (left) and to a private residence (right).

Valley. Syria rejected the agreement and so the settlement fell apart.

Fighting also continued over the control of the Al-Fatah, Palestine National Liberation Movement, between its leader, Yasser Arafat, chairman of the PLO, and two Syrian-backed rebels. A truce was arranged in 1983 through the mediation of Saudi Arabia and Syria. It allowed Arafat and four thousand of his supporters to leave Tripoli under United Nations protection. They went to the countries of Algeria, Tunisia, and the Yemen Arab Republic.

As the Israeli forces withdrew from Beirut, the multinational peacekeeping force of 2,000 French, 2,000 Italians, 1,600 Americans, and 1,000 British that had previously been in Beirut as part of the UN plan for the PLO evacuation was drawn into fighting Muslim militia forces. On October 23, 1983, in two incidents of suicide bombings involving trucks filled with explosives that were driven into military compounds, 241 United States and 58 French troops were killed in Beirut.

President Amin Gemayel talked to reporters before he spoke to the United Nations General Assembly in New York City.

In an attempt to find a resolution to the problems, Lebanese leaders from various factions met in Geneva in early November 1983. Agreement was reached on the need to give Muslims representation in the government in accord with their majority status in the population. However, by February 1984 the factional fighting was even more intense, and the Lebanese army and the multinational forces were unable to contain it.

Muslim members of the army defected to the militias rather than fight against their own people. The Sunni prime minister and the Cabinet resigned. The peacekeeping troops of the multinational forces were withdrawn.

THE UNITED NATIONS INTERVENES

In an effort to restore some kind of order, President Amin Gemayel called for a United Nations peacekeeping force to replace the multinational one. He abrogated the May 17, 1983 agreement with Israel and reconvened the National Reconciliation Conference. A government with equal representation of Christians and Muslims in the cabinet was approved by the National Assembly.

Finally in September 1984 Israel pledged to withdraw from Lebanon even though all Syrian forces did not leave. The cost of maintaining an Israeli force in Lebanon and the casualties sustained were factors in this decision. The PLO had been weakened from internal disputes and from refusal of the Shiites to allow the PLO to reestablish military bases in southern Lebanon where the Shiites held power. Withdrawal was not without incidents of fighting and repression on both sides; withdrawal of Israeli troops was completed ahead of schedule by June 10.

Shortly thereafter, Syria withdrew 10,000 to 12,000 troops from the valley, leaving 25,000 in place. The invasion of Lebanon by Israel had removed temporarily the threat of Palestinian fighters, at the cost of 654 Israeli lives.

CONTINUING CONFLICTS

Some of the reforms proposed by President Gemayel were not popular with the Christians. Fighting broke out between pro and anti-Gemayel Christian forces and between Christian and Muslim militias along the Green Line dividing east and west Beirut. In the south near Sidon, fighting had driven some sixty thousand Christian refugees to Jezzine. Also Christians launched attacks against the Palestinians who were returning to the camps in the south.

One event in June 1985 that had world attention focused on Beirut was the hijacking of a Trans World Airlines (TWA)

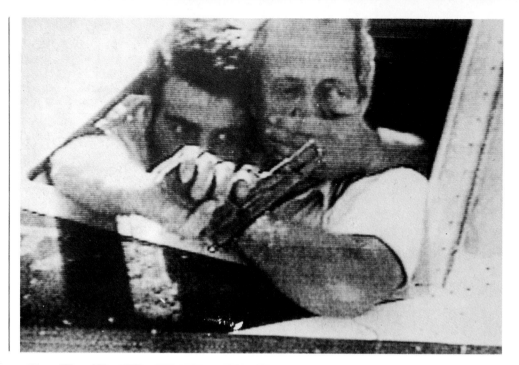

An armed terrorist holds a gun on the pilot of the hijacked Trans World Airlines plane in Beirut.

passenger aircraft by two Lebanese Shiite Muslims. These two reputedly were members of the *Hezbollah,* "the Party of God," with contacts in Iran. The flight had taken off from Athens, Greece, bound for Rome, Italy. The hijackers had it land three times in Beirut and twice in Algiers. One American passenger was beaten and killed. Some of the remaining Americans were taken off the plane and brought to a secret hiding place in Beirut. The hijackers demanded the release of 766 Lebanese prisoners in Israeli jails. The United States threatened to impose sanctions against Lebanon. President Assad of Syria negotiated the release of the prisoners. They were driven first to Damascus and then flown to a United States base in the Federal Republic of Germany. Individual Americans and Europeans were kidnapped at other times and held as prisoners against their will.

More attempts were made to adopt a security plan to stop the fighting and to change the constitution and certain government structures, but these failed. The United Nations peacekeeping force was involved in more fighting.

A sniper in Beirut (left) and the destruction caused by a bomb in July 1986 (right)

At the invitation of Muslim leaders, but with the president calling the move unconstitutional, some seventy-five hundred Syrian troops moved into Beirut in February 1987. However, the Syrians and their allies were not able to get the PLO forces out of Lebanon though they did drive them out of Beirut to camps near Sidon. Fighting between two Muslim militias continued in the southern suburbs of Beirut.

President Gemayel's term of office was scheduled to end on September 23, 1988, before the National Assembly was required to elect a new president. The political maneuverings, both inside and outside Lebanon, failed to settle on a possible new candidate.

Basically, a constitutional crisis occurred, leaving Lebanon with two governments claiming legitimacy. The Christian one held power in east Beirut; the predominantly Muslim one, in west Beirut. There was fear that this split might hasten a formal division of Lebanon into two nations.

The United Nations Secretary General Javier Perez de Cuellar called an emergency meeting of the UN Security Council to discuss the problem of a cease-fire in Lebanon. The emergency powers of the secretary general had been used on only two previous occasions. Reports were circulating that Syrian and Iranian-backed militias were planning to join the Syrian army to defeat the Lebanese army.

The Tripartite Arab Committee appointed by the Arab League at its Casablanca meeting in 1989 came up with another plan that did not involve withdrawal of Syrian troops. Because of diplomatic support for this plan from all the foreign countries having an interest in Lebanon, General Michel Aoun was forced to agree to a cease-fire that took effect on September 23, 1989.

The Lebanese National Assembly met in Taif, Saudi Arabia. The session was attended by thirty-one Christian deputies and thirty-one Muslim deputies of the seventy-three still surviving who had been elected in May 1972. A Charter of National Reconciliation (the Taif Agreement) was approved by fifty-eight of the sixty-two deputies. There was an attempt to balance political power between Christians and Muslims, but the Syrian army was to assist the new government with security plans for up to two years. The continued involvement of the Syrians was denounced by General Aoun as a betrayal of Lebanese sovereignty. The National Assembly met in November, ratified the Taif Agreement, and elected Rene Mouawad, a Maronite Christian, as president. Seventeen days later Mouawad was assassinated with a bomb. On November 24, fifty-two deputies of the National Assembly met and elected Elias Hrawi as president. General Aoun announced the dissolution of the National Assembly and declared the presidential election unconstitutional and void. In response, the new government announced that General Aoun had been dismissed as commander-in-chief of the Lebanese army.

Before his exile in France, General Michel Aoun appeared in Beirut.

Severe fighting for control of the Christian territory broke out in January 1990. There was fighting between General Aoun's forces and Lebanese forces under their new general Emile Lahud, between various Christian factions, and between Muslim militia. Again people fled from the fighting areas. Over nine hundred died, and three thousand were wounded. Armies inflicted new destruction on Lebanon. When Aoun failed to get foreign support, he finally halted the fighting between the Christian factions and indicated a willingness to accept a modified form of the Taif Agreement. General Aoun is now in exile in France.

The government of Syrian-backed President Hrawi began consolidating control and ordering the rival militias to turn over their armaments to the Lebanese army. In April 1991, the most powerful Christian, Druze, and Shiite militias gave the army 400 artillery pieces, 108 tanks, and 21 helicopters. The PLO refused to obey the order on grounds that its weapons were used against the Israelis and not Lebanese factions.

Many people were forced to move to another location in Beirut after Israeli attacks destroyed their homes.

Between January 1 and June 3, 1991, the Israelis had launched thirteen separate air strikes killing and wounding persons in southern Lebanon. Also during the year Israeli commandos had stormed a PLO base north of their security zone, the Lebanese territory that Israel has held since 1985 along the Israeli border as a safeguard for Israeli citizens from attacks. In July, Lebanese forces seized control of Palestinian bases near Sidon and disarmed the Palestinians.

Lebanon has joined other Middle Eastern countries in accepting the United States proposal for an Arab-Israeli Peace Conference. The foreign minister has announced that at the conference Lebanon would call for the immediate implementation of the United Nations Resolution 425, which instructed Israel to withdraw its forces from southern Lebanon. Iraq, during the Gulf War, protested against the lack of enforcement of this United Nations Resolution. However, Israel has announced that it will not withdraw from the security zone along the Israeli-Lebanese border that it established in 1985 to protect its citizens from the Palestinian raids.

President Elias Hrawi

On May 22, 1991, President Hrawi signed a treaty with Syria under which Syria recognized Lebanon as a separate and independent state for the first time since the two countries became independent from France in 1943. However, the Israelis and the Lebanese Christians warned that the treaty was, in effect, an annexation of Lebanon. The treaty provides for joint commissions to coordinate the policies of the two nations for defense, internal security, and economic and foreign affairs.

The government still has much work to do in rebuilding the country. Internal threats still exist with a population split into groups and used to fighting to achieve their goals. External problems have not been resolved, with the Israelis still holding Lebanese territory and raiding over the border. Lebanon's alliance with Syria has raised concerns both within and outside the country. Nevertheless, the government's attempts to regain control over the factions within its borders provide hope for an end to what has been one of the longest and bloodiest civil wars of the twentieth century.

Parliament Square in Beirut

Chapter 7

GOVERNMENT, FAMILY, AND CULTURE

While the governmental structures may change, it is likely that the family and group loyalties that bind people together will continue to be strong. The bitter fighting that has gone on for such a long period of time, however, increases the difficulty of people working together, even if a cease-fire can be maintained over time.

GOVERNMENT

Lebanon is a republic with a parliamentary system of government. Under its constitution of 1926, which has been amended on several occasions, no part of the nation's territory may be sold or given away. All Lebanese are equal under the law. An agreement established in 1943, called the National Pact, said Lebanon was an Arab country, and that there would be a fair representation of religions in government. There are protections for personal freedom and freedom of the press. Religious communities are entitled to maintain their own schools, provided they conform to requirements for public instruction specified by law. Lebanese citizens who are twenty-one years old are eligible to vote.

Legislative power is vested in one house originally called the Chamber of Deputies but renamed the National Assembly. While its ninety-nine seats were allocated to give fifty-three to Christians and forty-five to Muslims, under the Taif Agreement of 1989 the seats were increased to 108—equally divided between Christians and Muslims. Members are considered to represent the nation as a whole and do not need to follow the directions of their constituencies. To serve in the National Assembly, members must be over twenty-five years of age, with full political and civil rights, and be literate. The normal term is for four years, but as in other parliamentary systems terms can be shorter if the government resigns or is voted out of office.

The president is elected by a two-thirds majority of the members of the National Assembly for a six-year term. The president can be reelected only after a lapse of another six years. The president selects the prime minister and other ministers who execute the laws. The ministers do not need to be members of the National Assembly, although they are responsible to it and have access to debates held there. The president can initiate laws and demand further debate on laws that have been adopted. By tradition, the president must be a Maronite; the prime minister, a Sunni Muslim; and the speaker of the National Assembly, a Shiite. The rest of the offices are supposed to be appointed so that other groups also have representation.

Over twenty major political parties represent the many groups within Lebanon. Parties splinter and reform around new issues and leaders. Many of the parties have special affinities to foreign countries.

The judicial system was modeled after the French system. There are fifty-six single-judge courts that try both civil and criminal cases. Eleven courts of appeal, each consisting of three judges, include a president and public prosecutor. There are four courts of cassation that deal with civil, commercial, and criminal cases. These courts must have at least three judges with a requirement that at least two must be councillors and have the power to retry a case instead of sending it back to the lower court.

A Council of State deals with administrative matters, and the Court of Justice deals with matters affecting the security of the nation. In addition, there are Islamic, Christian, and Jewish religious courts that deal with issues of personal status such as marriage, death, and inheritance. Lebanon's civil courts do not handle these matters at all. Even though Lebanon has a well-developed legal system and a high proportion of lawyers, a large number of disputes are still handled by feuds and fighting.

FAMILY

The family unit is extremely important in Lebanon. Since intermarriage with other religious groups is discouraged, the family and the religious community reinforce each other. In political power, business opportunities, and personal relationships, family backing is important. Employers give preference to family members in hiring. Wealthy family members, whether they have moved to the city or even to another country,

The family is important to the Lebanese.

are expected to help support less prosperous family members. In the past, the three-generation extended families (grandparents through grandchildren) may have lived under one roof as one household. Now even though they may live in separate homes, the kinship tie is strong.

Where the family unit is so important, marriage is a decision of great consequence, not only for the partners but also for the families. Therefore it is not surprising that the whole family gives considerable attention to the arrangements. Although the feelings of the parties involved are taken into account because harmony is desired, economic and political factors may be as important as romantic attractions.

Women in Beirut in Western-style clothing

Children are very important to the family system and are taught to put family interests ahead of their own and to respect, especially, the father. The mother is usually the more compassionate one. Traditional roles for women that are customary throughout the Middle East have resulted in different treatment of boys and girls; however, these attitudes have been changing. In Beirut, middle and upper-class women have had the opportunities of university educations and professional work. Women of poorer classes may work as waitresses and nurses. Women obtained the right to vote and to hold office in 1953.

College students learning oil technology

EDUCATION

Primary education had been available free in Lebanese schools since 1960. Literacy has been the highest of countries in the Middle East. Private schools provide most of the secondary and university education. Except for schools that receive government financial aid and are therefore supervised by government inspectors, most of the private schools are almost entirely independent of the government.

Primary education begins when a student is six years old and continues for five years. Next the student can go to a four-year intermediate school or a three-year secondary school. A technical education from the National School of Arts and Crafts provides four years in electronics, mechanics, and architectural and industrial drawing, among other subjects. There are public vocational schools that provide training for lower levels.

The campus of American University in Beirut

University education is supplied by at least six universities, including one opened in mid-1988 that is run by a Maronite order. The American University in Beirut has a long tradition in training leaders in the Middle East. There are special schools for teacher training and agriculture.

HEALTH AND WELFARE

Lebanon had a large number of medical personnel and hospital facilities that were adequate under normal circumstances. However the war placed a great burden on these facilities and overwhelmed them with casualties that interrupted normal treatment. A book by Leila Richards, an American doctor working near Sayda in the 1980s, entitled *The Hills of Sidon*, describes what it was like to work in a hospital during the Lebanese conflict.

A child plays with a makeshift toy in a bombed-out area.

Under normal conditions the public facilities had been supplemented by religious and ethnic-sponsored services. The health of the Lebanese people was considered good because of the satisfactory diet, the climate, and the high standard of living. Unfortunately the war changed some of these conditions, making food costly and sometimes very difficult to obtain, and the cost of living and unemployment rose. The stress and strain of living under war conditions affected even those not wounded or injured in the fighting.

Housing, which was a problem even before the civil war, has become even more difficult with the destruction of property and the dislocation of people. Property rights have been violated in the

Handwoven carpets (left) and hammered brass ware (right)

chaotic situation throughout the country. Although the government has been sensitive to the need for low-cost housing and has established a housing bank to make housing loans, rehabilitation of the combat areas will require a major effort.

CULTURAL LIFE

Lebanon has had a long tradition of artistic and literary talent. In the nineteenth century, the Lebanese were among the first to promote an Arabic literary reawakening. Writers such as Kahlil Gibran, Georges Shehade, and Michel Chiha have been translated

A temple in Baalbek built by the Romans

and appreciated by international readers. The universities in Beirut were the center of cultural life. Beirut was home to several museums, libraries, learned societies, and research institutions.

The Baalbek International Festival has the spectacular ancient ruins as a backdrop. International opera, ballet, symphony, and drama companies from many nationalities used to come to Beirut. Folk art in the form of song, dance, poetry, and crafts was encouraged. Many Lebanese artists worked to create a larger audience in their homeland and in Europe for classical Arabic music and drama. The fighting has interfered with much of this cultural revival.

Beirut boasted Arabic, English, French, and Armenian publications and newspapers, in addition to foreign newspapers and magazines. Before the civil war, the low cost of movies and the wide variety of films made movie-going a national hobby. A 1991 Cannes Film Festival prize, an important international award, was given to Lebanese director Maroun Bagdadi for *Hors de Vie (Out of Life)*. Television was supplied by Beirut private companies and by Egyptian and Syrian TV stations. The government-operated radio station broadcasts programs in Arabic, French, English, and Armenian. With the war, many secret radio stations began broadcasting to bring news and propaganda of the various groups to the Lebanese population, which was well supplied with transistor radios.

This country, once so prosperous and forward looking, has been damaged to a great extent by the long, bitter fighting. The reconstruction of the country will be a major undertaking, but Lebanon, so often battered in the past with conquering forces, has always accepted the challenge to rebuild.

A busy commercial street in
Beirut photographed before
the civil war in 1975
(above) and damaged
buildings after the
cease-fire (left) in 1976

Chapter 8

THE ECONOMY—FROM BOOM TO BUST

The heirs of the great Phoenician traders had built Lebanon into a center for trade and financial services before the Civil War of 1975 began. The gross domestic product increased at an annual rate of from 6 percent to 6.5 percent between 1964 and 1974. Income per person was estimated to be $1,300 in 1974—one of the highest among the developing countries. After the Israeli invasion of 1982, however, the gross domestic product figure declined steadily. The uncertainty of conditions in Lebanon led to the shift of banking business to financial centers in the gulf states, and it is unlikely that Lebanon will be able to regain this business.

From 1984 to 1987 there was still some hope that reconstruction programs might be implemented to rebuild the country, but with the political situation deteriorating, the economic picture worsened. High unemployment, shifts of population, and postponement of the reconstruction projects led to depression that

Smoke rises up from a burning section of Beirut (top).
Even after areas had been completely destroyed (left),
it was unsafe because mines were sometimes found
in the ruins. Many Lebanese, like this woman above
in New York state, have sought refuge outside their
country.

brought the country to near collapse. Many left the country to establish themselves in Cyprus, the United States, or Australia. For those in Lebanon, strikes and demonstrations by citizens in all parts of the country indicated their anger at the increasing poverty and continued fighting.

The government has been trying to plan for the country through the Council for Development and Reconstruction. A list of needs has been presented to the World Bank and to foreign countries who are likely to give aid. However, the fighting that continues makes it difficult for the government to wisely spend the money that it already has been given.

LABOR FORCE

The population of Lebanon has declined from a high estimated to be 3,100,000 in 1974, making the country one of the most densely populated in the Middle East, to a low estimated in 1984 to be 1,644,000. There have been estimates of from 30,000 to 60,000 killed in the Civil War of 1975-76, more thousands killed in 1978, 19,085 killed as the result of the Israeli invasion in 1982 — and still the slaughter continues.

Many Lebanese had emigrated since the 1890s, and by 1960 it was thought that 2,500,000 Lebanese or those of Lebanese descent were living outside the country. The money these people sent from foreign countries to their families amounted to about 35 percent of Lebanon's gross national product. Monthly remittances ranging from $75,000,000 to $200,000,000, depending on the economic conditions where people work, have been sent into the country.

Farmland in the Bekaa Valley

The civil war encouraged more Lebanese to join families abroad, which resulted in a "brain drain" of educated and skilled workers while leaving a pool of unemployed persons. Also the Israeli invasion caused thousands of Syrians and Palestinians who were working in Lebanon to flee the country. Employment dropped, mostly in the fields of industry, construction, transportation, and communication. However, estimates for mid-1986 suggested that unemployment was close to 50 percent. Most of the unemployed were engaged in paramilitary or black market activities.

AGRICULTURE

Because of the large forest and mountainous areas, only 23 percent of the land is being cultivated, with an additional 17 percent considered possible for farming. The coastal strip is very

*Fresh figs, grapes and other fruit
for sale (above) in a market, and a fine
display of various types of olives in a shop.*

fertile. Olives, citrus fruits, and bananas are grown here. Grapes,
cotton, and onions are grown in the north. The Bekaa Valley is the
cereal growing center. Farms are very small, and in the mountain
areas may be in several widely spaced holdings. Agriculture,
which before the civil war contributed 9 percent to the gross
domestic product, was down to 5 percent in 1985. People have
moved away from the countryside to the cities.

The government has adopted a number of strategies to improve
agriculture. In 1963 the "Green Plan" was put into effect to
reclaim land for farming. Also in 1980 the United Nations Food
and Agricultural Organization proposed plans to protect grazing
lands, to preserve cultivated areas, to prevent housing from being
built on agricultural land, and to increase forests from 7 percent to
20 percent of the total land area. The International Fund for
Agricultural Development outlined a plan to help small farmers
through improvement of bombed and inadequate roads,

Harvesting sugar beets

replacement of livestock lost in the years of fighting, distribution of apple boxes for cold storage, and provisions of agricultural credit.

The wheat crop varies a good deal according to the growing conditions. Citrus crops have generally increased, while sugar beet and tobacco growing are down. One crop that benefited from the fighting and lack of security was hemp from which hashish is made and which provided high profits. However, the war conditions interfered with the usual patterns of agricultural labor and made it difficult to get crops to market. Farmers took heavy losses. Some Arab countries were unwilling to buy crops from Lebanon because it was suspected that the crops were being grown in Israel and then marketed through Lebanon.

A cement factory

INDUSTRY

Mineral resources of Lebanon are fairly limited. There are minor deposits of high-grade iron ore, asphalt, coal, and phosphates. Lignite and some iron ore have been smelted in Beirut. Building-stone quarries, high-quality sand (suitable for glass manufacture), and lime have been found. Hopes for significant petroleum reserves have not yet found fulfillment.

Lebanon participated in the petroleum industry through two important pipelines from the Iraqi and Saudi Arabian fields. One terminated near Tripoli; the other at Zahrani, near Sayda. Oil refineries were built in Lebanon at the pipeline terminals. Both refineries have been subject to the problems of the supplying countries and oil prices. At home, bomb blasts to the pipeline to Tripoli and Israeli bombing of the refinery near Sidon interrupted

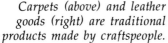
Carpets (above) and leather goods (right) are traditional products made by craftspeople.

the flow. In 1986 the government took over the operation of the Zahrani refinery when the private company gave notice that it was stopping operations because of financial losses.

Manufacturing has long been a major industry in Lebanon in comparison with most other Middle East states. In 1974 manufacturing accounted for 16 percent of the national income and gave jobs to over 120,000. Yet in the civil war, plants were damaged or destroyed.

The Israeli invasion in 1982 destroyed more of the major industrial units and left fewer than 50 percent of the textile factories in operation.

In addition to the problems that fighting created, the war conditions resulted in shortages of skilled labor. In 1986 it was estimated that the industrial sector was operating at only 40 percent of capacity with textiles, leather goods, and finished wood products the most important industries.

The Bank of Lebanon in 1977

BANKING AND FINANCE

Before the civil war, Lebanon was a center of banking for the Middle East. Many foreign firms had their Middle Eastern headquarters in Beirut. The lack of restriction on the free movement of goods and the boom in oil revenues added to the money that found its way into the country. When the hazards of war and fighting complicated business in Lebanon, much of these reserves were transferred to banks in the gulf area.

During 1987 the Lebanese currency, the pound, lost 82 percent of its value in international trade. Prices rose by 420 percent. The failure of the National Assembly to elect a president in September 1988 brought a further decline in the exchange rate for the Lebanese currency that continued to slip, with some variations, depending on the war news.

The Lebanese tourist industry would like peace in the area so vacationers would return to the St. George Hotel (left) and the Yacht Club (below).

TOURISM AND COMMUNICATION

Before the civil war, first-class hotels with swimming pools attracted visitors to Beirut through the busy international airport. Tourism accounted for 20 percent of the gross national product before the war, but by 1977 this had declined to 7.4 percent. The Israeli invasion and the shelling around Beirut has wrecked the tourist industry.

The Middle East Airlines (MEA) had been the nation's largest nongovernmental employer before the civil war. After the Israeli invasion and the closing of Beirut airport, the airline went from a profitable operation to one sustaining severe losses. The opening of an airport at Halat by private developers so that Christians would not have to fly into Muslim-held territory caused additional problems when the government refused to recognize the new airport and the Christian militia closed down the Beirut airport with shell fire. Beirut airport was reopened after the

A plane of Middle East Airlines at Beirut International Airport

government gave assurance the Halat airport would be given official status.

Who controls the ports of the coastal cities has been a matter of concern, not just historically but also in the present-day fighting. Whoever had control over the ports also had control over the customs fees that could be collected in their operation. Because the area in which the ports were located was sometimes in the hands of the militia, the government lost out on customs receipts that it had expected to obtain.

Lebanon had a strong economy before the civil war in 1975. Whether the country will be able to recover from the severe problems of inflation, the devaluation of its currency, and the war damage to its industries and trade will depend on what kind of political settlement can be worked out to keep the country at peace and the factions willing to work together to build a stable and strong nation.

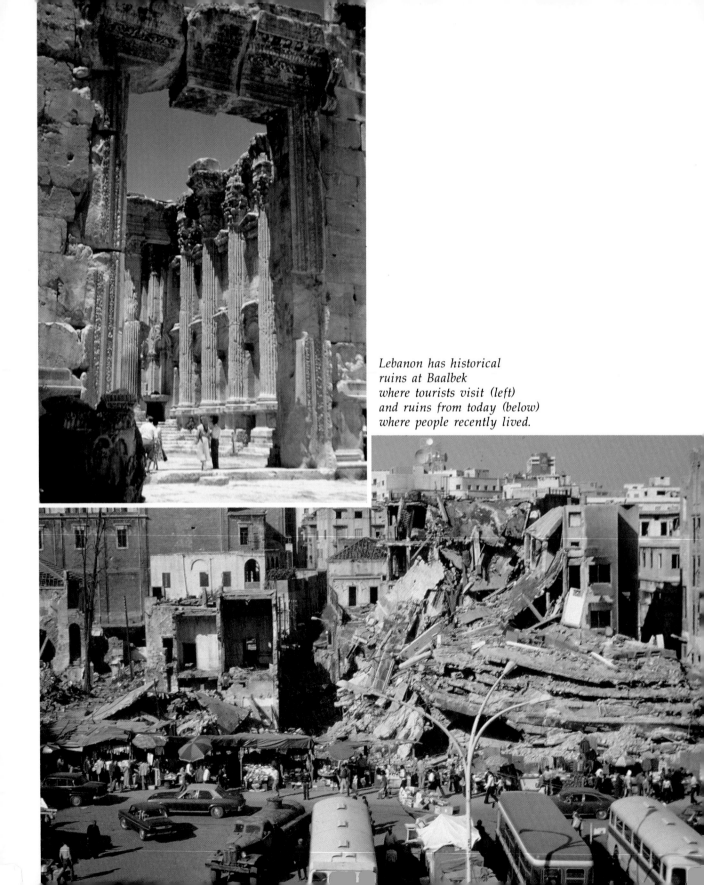

Lebanon has historical
ruins at Baalbek
where tourists visit (left)
and ruins from today (below)
where people recently lived.

Chapter 9

LEBANON OF THE PAST, PRESENT, AND FUTURE

What is it like to live in a beautiful but war-torn country like Lebanon? This question could have been asked of the Phoenicians who had to balance the Egyptian and Mesopotamian powers. It could have been asked of the people living between the Greek and Persian Empires. It could have been put to the inhabitants of the eastern Mediterranean countries caught in the battles between the Crusaders and the Muslims. Certainly, it can be raised with the Lebanese of the present who are still struggling with external influences and internal factions.

A civilian in Lebanon had to know how to keep necessities and food supplies so that it would not be necessary to go out when the fighting closed down the marketplace. One had to keep a sharp lookout for the enemy. One had to learn to sleep and keep one's

A child (above left) in the Bekaa Valley and women (above right) in Beirut know the hardships of war and war damage (below).

Children in the south flash the victory sign.

wits when bombs burst in the air. One had to learn how to get through checkpoints of the military if travel was attempted in the country. One had to learn how to raise children in such an environment if they could not be sent out of the country to relatives.

Children learned to play games like lighting a firecracker under a toy car to see it explode. They learned to admire the fighters who were protecting their families. They learned to hate the enemy. Civil wars and unrest are hard on the future generations of leaders, and Lebanon has undergone one of the longest and bloodiest of wars and unrest in the twentieth century.

To succeed at the costly task of rebuilding the country, Lebanon needs a stable government and factions willing to work together so that investment in reconstruction will make sense. Many living in this war-torn country, many Lebanese watching from foreign countries, and many friends of the Lebanese want to see a return to peace and prosperity.

Ruins of a Roman temple built about two thousand years ago show
the fluted columns (above) and bas-relief sculpture (below).

These rock formations off the coast of Beirut are called Pigeon Rocks.

The Lebanese have a proud heritage. Many times throughout their history, these people have created a center of culture, education, and art. The Lebanese have been good traders and entrepreneurs from the days of the Phoenician sailors to the twentieth-century bankers who attracted international wealth to the shores of the country. The beauty of the sea and mountains of Lebanon has drawn not only Cleopatra but also tourists in modern times. The country has provided a home for many groups fleeing the tyranny of neighboring rulers.

Lebanon has won the independence it fought hard to achieve. To hold on to this independence, the Lebanese will have the hard task of balancing the interests of the many groups living within its boundaries and dealing with the power politics of the Middle East and the world.

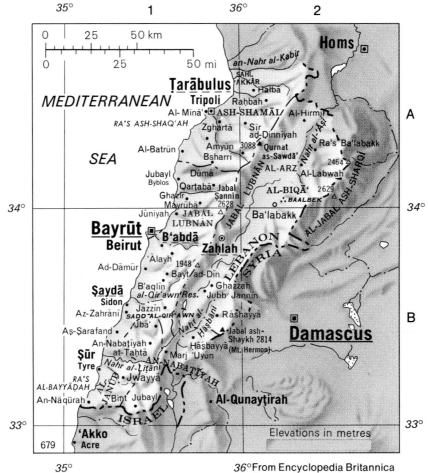

LEBANON

From Encyclopedia Britannica
© 1991 by Rand McNally R.L. 91-S-251

MAP KEY

Ad-Damur	B1	Bayt ad-Din (mountain peak)	B1	MEDITERRANEAN SEA	A1, B1
AL-ARZ	A2	Beirut (Bayrut)	B1	Nahr al-Asi (Orontes River)	A2
Al-Batrun	A1	Bint Jubayl	B1	Nahr al Hasbani (river)	B1
AL-BIQA (Bekaa Valley)	A2	Bsharri	A1	Nahr al-Litani (Litani River)	B1
Al-Hirmil	A2	Byblos (Jubayl)	A1	Qartaba	A1
AL-JANUB	B1	Duma	A1	Qurnat as-Sawda (mountain peak)	A2
Al-Labwah	A2	Ghazir	A1	Rahbah	A2
Al-Mina	A1	Ghazzah	B1	RA'S AL-BAYYADAH	B1
al-Qir'awn Res. (reservoir)	B1	Halba	A2	RA'S ASH-SHAQ'AH	A1
Alayh	B1	Hasbayya	B1	Ra's Ba'labakk	A2
Amyun	A1	Jabal ash-Shaykh (Mt. Hermon)	B1	Rashayya	B1
An-Nabatiyah at-Tahta	B1	JABAL LUBNAN (Lebanon		SADD AL-QIR AWN (Karaoum Dam)	B1
AN-NABATIYAH	B1	Mountains)	A1, A2	SAHL AKKAR (Plain of Akkar)	A1, A2
An-Naqurah	B1	Jabal Sannin (mountain)	B1	Sayda (Sidon)	B1
As-Sarafand	B1	Jazzin	B1	Sidon (Sayda)	B1
ASH-SHAMAL	A1, A2	Jba	B1	Sir ad-Dinniyah	A2
Az-Zahrani	B1	Jubayl (Byblos)	A1	Sur (Tyre)	B1
BAALBEK (ruin)	A2	Jubb' Jannin	B1	Tarabulus (Tripoli)	A1
B'abda	B1	Juniyah	B1	Tripoli (Tarabulus)	A1
Ba'labakk	B2	Jwayya	B1	Tyre (Sur)	B1
B'aqlin	B1	Marj Uyun	B1	Zahlah	B1
Bayrut (Beirut)	B1	Mayruba	A1	Zgharta	A1

A sumptuous spread of Lebanese food

MINI-FACTS AT A GLANCE

GENERAL INFORMATION

Official Name: al-Jumhuriyah al-Lubananiyah (Republic of Lebanon)

Capital: Beirut

Government: Lebanon is a multiparty republic with one legislative house (National Assembly). The president is the chief of state and the prime minister is the chief of government. The prime minister is selected by the president. By agreement the president is always a Maronite Christian, the prime minister a Sunni Muslim, and the speaker of the National Assembly a Shiite Muslim.

The 108 members of the National Assembly were last elected in 1972; the Assembly elections are postponed until 1994. The 1989 Taif Agreement increased the number of members from 99 to 108—divided equally among Christian and Muslim deputies. Lebanese citizens, 21 years and older, are eligible to vote. For administrative purposes the country is divided in five provinces, each headed by a governor.

The judicial system is modeled after the French system. There are four courts of cassation. In addition to judicial courts, Islamic, Christian, and Jewish religious courts deal with matters of personal affairs such as marriage, death, and inheritance.

Religion: The last religious breakdown of population is available for 1932 when Maronite Christians had a majority. In the 1990s it was estimated that Muslims constitute a majority. The largest religious groups are Shiite Muslims, Maronite Christians (affiliated with the Roman Catholic church), Sunni Muslims, Druze (a sect that broke away from Islam in the Middle Ages), Greek Orthodox, Greek Catholic, and Armenian Christians. There is also a very small Jewish minority.

Ethnic Composition: Almost 90 percent of the people are Arabs. Lebanese form the largest ethnic majority (83 percent); followed by Palestinians (10 percent, refugees from the Arab-Israel wars), Armenians (5 percent), and Syrians, Kurds, and others.

Language: Arabic is the official language and is spoken by almost all. Many educated urban people also speak English. French is widely used as a second language. Some minorities also speak Armenian, Kurdish, and Turkish. Many people speak three or four languages.

National Flag: The national flag, introduced in 1943, consists of two horizontal red stripes, separated by a white stripe that is twice as wide. At the center is a cedar tree in green and brown. The cedar tree, symbolizing holiness, eternity, and peace, is native to the area and is mentioned several times in the Bible.

National Anthem: "Kulluna lil watan lil'ula lil'alam" ("All of Us for the Country, Glory, Flag")

Money: The Lebanese pound, or livre libanaise (LL), is a paper currency of 100 piasters. In early 1992 one Lebanese pound was equal to $0.001138 in U.S. currency.

Weights and Measures: The metric system is the legal standard.

Membership in International Organizations: Lebanon is a member of the Arab Fund for Economic and Social Development, the Arab Monetary Fund, the Council of Arab Economic Unity, and the Islamic Development Bank.

Population: Population estimates in 1989 were 3.3 million; 81 percent urban and 19 percent rural. Density in 1990 was 751 persons per sq. mi. (290 persons per sq km).

Cities:

Beirut	1,100,000
Tripoli	240,000
Sidon	110,000
Tyre	60,000
Zahleh	55,000

GEOGRAPHY

Area: 4,015 sq. mi. (10,399 sq km)

Coastline: 130 mi. (209 km)

Border: Lebanon is bordered on the north and east by Syria, on the south by Israel, and on the west by the Mediterranean Sea.

Land: The coastal plains are narrow along the Mediterranean Sea. East of the plains, rugged Mount Lebanon region extends for about 100 mi. (160 km). A grove of ancient and famed cedar trees survives in the northern mountains. The Anti-Lebanon mountains run along the country's eastern border. Between the Lebanon and Anti-Lebanon ranges is situated the Bekaa Valley—an extremely fertile area about 10 mi. (16 km) wide and 80 mi. (129 km) long.

Climate: Lebanon's wide range of elevation and westerly winds influence its climate greatly. The typical Mediterranean climate has warm and dry summers and rainy and cool winters. By Middle Eastern standards, the rainfall is abundant. Rainfall varies from 35 in. (90 cm) along the coast, to 50 in. (125 cm) on the western slopes of the mountains, to less than 15 in. (28 cm) in the Bekaa Valley. Most of the rain falls between November and March. Summer is humid especially along the coast. At higher elevations snow falls occur from December to May. The average annual temperatures in Beirut ranges from 55° F (13° C) in winter to 82° F (28° C) in summer.

Highest Point: Qurnat as-Sawda, 10,115 ft. (3,083 m)

Lowest Point: Sea level along the coast

Rivers: There are very few rivers. The Litani is the major river. The Orontes River *(Nahr al-Asi)* reaches the Mediterranean Sea after flowing through Syria and Turkey. Natural springs abound on the western slopes of the Lebanon Mountains; these springs provide water at heights up to 5,000 ft. (1,500 m).

Forests: Almost 8 percent of land is under forests. Olive and fig trees grow on the lower slopes, while cedar, maple, juniper, fir, cypress, oak, and Aleppo pine trees are found on higher slopes. During World War I, almost 60 percent of the trees of Lebanon were cut, primarily for the railroads. The National Preservation Park was created in 1986 to preserve wooded areas and animals.

Wildlife: Gazelles, rabbits, and jackals are abundant. Mice, squirrels, gerbils, lizards, and snakes are the common rodents and reptiles. Nightingales, thrushes, and many other song birds are native to Lebanon. Other birds include pigeons, vultures, golden eagles, flamingos, pelicans, ducks, herons, storks, and partridges. Hunting has killed off most wild mammals. It is estimated that by 1987 the Arabian gazelle and Anatolian leopard were extinct.

Greatest Distance: North to south—120 mi. (193 km)
East to west—50 mi. (80 km)

ECONOMY AND INDUSTRY

Agriculture: Some 25 percent of land is available for agriculture, and some 20 percent of the population is employed in agriculture. Wheat, barley, maize, lentils, vegetables (potatoes, cucumbers, onions, cabbages, eggplants, green beans, peas, carrots), watermelons, lemons, limes, bananas, apples, cherries, grapes, oranges, peaches, sugar beets, tobacco, and olives are the chief agricultural products. Production of opium poppies and hemp increased in the early 1980s. Domestic animals include goats, sheep, horses, donkeys, mules, and cattle.

Mining: Mineral resources are fairly limited. Salt and gypsum are the chief minerals; there are minor deposits of iron ore, asphalt, coal, and phosphates. Petroleum refining is important for the economy. There are two major oil pipelines running from the Iraqi and Saudi Arabian oil fields. There are two oil refineries.

Manufacturing: Cement, chemicals, electric appliances, furniture, textiles, paper and paperboard, and food processing are Lebanon's chief industries.

Transportation: In the early 1990s, much of Lebanon's transport system was destroyed. There are some 650 mi. (400 km) of railroad tracks. The total road length is about 11,900 mi. (7,400 km), out of which about 85 percent are paved. Beirut is the chief port and also has an international airport; there is another airport at Halat. Bicycles, private taxis, and city buses provide transportation within cities.

Communication: There are some 40 daily newspapers published in Lebanon. *Al-*

Anwar and *An-Nahar* are the two most important daily newspapers. The government-operated radio stations broadcast programs in Arabic, French, English, and Armenian. In the early 1990s there was one radio per 1.3 persons, one television set per 3.5 persons, and one telephone per 18 persons.

Trade: Lebanon has been a major trade and financial center of the Middle East since the early 19th century. Chief imports are consumer goods, machinery and transport equipment, and petroleum products. Major import sources are Italy, Turkey, France, Germany, United States, Romania, and Saudi Arabia. Major exports are jewelry, clothing, pharmaceutical, and metal products. Chief export destinations are Saudi Arabia, Switzerland, Jordan, Kuwait, and the United States.

EVERYDAY LIFE

Health and Social Welfare: Medical services are provided mainly by private agencies. Public welfare for the poor, sick, or needy is provided by the family and charitable institutions rather than the state. A social security fund covers the medical expenses of the workers.

Education: Low-cost government schools are available to all. Primary education (free since 1960) begins at the age of six years and continues for five years. Education is compulsory by law for five years, and almost 95 percent of the children attend school. Private schools are expensive, but the quality of education is higher. Technical education in electronics, mechanics, and architecture is provided by the National School of Arts and Crafts. There are several universities, such as the Lebanese University, Saint Joseph University, the Beirut Arab University, and the American University of Beirut (a private university). Many students study abroad in foreign universities. In the late 1980s the literacy rate was about 77 percent—one of the highest in the Middle East.

Holidays:

New Year's Day, January 1
Feast of Saint Maron, February 9
Arab League Day, March 22
May Day, May 1
Independence Day, November 22
Christmas, December 25
Evacuation Day, December 31

Christian religious holidays are Good Friday, Easter Monday, and All Saints' Day. Muslim religious holidays include 'Id al-Fitr, 'Id ad-'Adha, and Milad an-Nabi. Ramadan is the most important Muslim holiday — it involves a month of fasting during the day.

Culture: The tradition of artistic and literary talent has existed in Lebanon for centuries. Writers such as Khalil Gibran have been translated and appreciated by international readers. Traditional Arab, Western, and folk music is popular. Before the civil war many international opera, ballet, symphony, and drama companies used to come to Beirut. Lebanese are famous for their silver and brass ware, jewelry, glassware, calligraphy, pottery, and needlework.

Housing: Traditional houses are made of limestone walls and tiled or thatched roofs. Modern housing and high-rise apartment buildings are becoming common in most of the cities. Most of the city houses have a chlorinated water system for the kitchen, and a separate water system for the rest of the house. In rural areas, more than one generation live together in the family house. Elders are respected greatly. Large number of Palestinians live in overcrowded refugee camps; these camps lack sanitation and clean drinking water facilities. Recently the government has established a housing bank to facilitate low-cost housing in the war-torn areas.

Food: A typical Lebanese main meal can last up to two hours and is eaten during the afternoon. The average meal has more bread, fruit, vegetables, and rice than meat of any kind. Lamb is the most widely used meat; pork is forbidden for Muslims by the *Koran*. The food is often spicy and hot. Cheese, olives, *hummus* (a paste of chick-peas, sesame seeds, and garlic), and round, flat bread are the basic foods. Arabic coffee, strong and thick, and a strong liquor *(arak)* are the popular drinks.

Sports and Recreation: Soccer is the most popular Lebanese sport. Swimming and beach activities are popular during the summer. Other popular games are basketball, skiing, table tennis, and volleyball. Moviegoing is popular, especially in cities. Visiting friends and relatives is the most common recreation.

IMPORTANT DATES

3000 B.C. — Phoenicians first move to the Lebanon region from the south

1100 B.C. — First Assyrian expedition comes to Lebanon

612 B.C.—Assyrian Empire is overthrown by the Medes

332 B.C.—Alexander the Great conquers Lebanon

64 B.C.—Territory of Phoenicia comes under the Roman Empire

A.D. 325—Christianity is introduced into Lebanon area under Constantine the Great

349—Earthquake hits Berytus

395—Roman Emperor Theodosius the Great dies; Lebanon region becomes part of the Byzantine Empire

552—Much of Berytus is destroyed by an earthquake and a tidal wave

560—Great fire kills about 30,000 people in Berytus

600—Muslims from neighboring regions occupy Lebanon

636—General Khalid ibn al-Walid wins the Battle of Yarmuk

660—Muawiyah becomes caliph

750—Umayyads are finally defeated

878—Deputy governor of Egypt takes control of Palestine and parts of Syria

1095-1291—Crusaders from Europe invade the region of Lebanon

1120—Maan family comes to Lebanon to defend against the Crusaders

1187—Saladin, a Muslim general, captures Jerusalem

1348—The Black Death (plague) kills thousands of citizens in Damascus, Syria

1516—Ottoman Turks conquer Lebanon

1697 — Last of the Maan family leader dies without an heir

1763 — Maronites enter into full communion with the Roman Catholic church

1840 — London Treaty is signed

1842 — Partition of Lebanon sets off religious wars

1860 — Druze massacre some of the Maronites

1861 — Territory of Mt. Lebanon is established as an autonomous district of the Ottoman Empire

1866 — The American University of Beirut is founded

1875 — Saint Joseph's University (French) is established in Beirut

1918 — Great Britain and France occupy Lebanon at the end of World War I

1920 — Boundaries of Greater Lebanon are drawn after World War I; Lebanon is administered by France under a League of Nations mandate until 1941

1922 — France starts preparing Lebanon for independence

1926 — The constitution is promulgated and Lebanon becomes a republic

1933 — *Al-Nahar,* an Arabic newspaper, is founded

1940 — Emile Edde is elected president by the Chamber of Deputies

1941 — An armistice is signed in Acre

1943 — Lebanon becomes completely independent; the National Pact agreement is established

1945 — Lebanon becomes a member of the United Nations and the Arab League

1946 — Last of the French troops are withdrawn

1948 — The state of Israel is established; Lebanon joins in fighting against the new state; a large number of Palestinian refugees from Israel settle in Lebanon

1949 — Lebanon, Egypt, Jordan, and Syria each signs an armistice with Israel mediated by the United Nations

1952 — General strike forces President al-Khuri to resign; Camille Chamoun is elected president

1953 — Women obtain the right to vote and to hold office

1955 — World Bank grants Lebanon a loan of $27 million for the Litani River project

1956 — Israel, Britain, and France attack the Suez Canal

1958 — Lebanon announces its refusal to join either Syria and Egypt (United Arab Republic), or Iraq and Jordan (Arab Federation); Muslim Lebanese rebel against government rule; on request from President Chamoun, the United States sends marines to Lebanon

1959 — Commercial television service is started; *Al-Anwar*, an Arabic newspaper, is founded

1960 — Primary education becomes free in government schools

1961 — Unsuccessful attempt by the military to overthrow the Lebanese government is crushed

1963 — Government sponsors the "Green Plan" to reclaim land for farming

1964 — Palestine Liberation Organization (PLO) is founded; its headquarters are established in Beirut; Charles Helou is elected president of Lebanon

1966 — Lebanon faces a massive financial crisis

1967 — As the result of Arab-Israeli War, additional Palestinian refugees from Israel settle in Lebanon

1968 — Israeli commandos raid Beirut airport

1969 — PLO attacks Israel from bases in Lebanon

1970 — Refugees flee from Jordan to Lebanon

1971 — Palestinian *fedayeen* ("martyrs") are expelled from Jordan

1972 — General elections take place; (next elections are planned for 1994)

1973 — Arab-Israeli War takes place

1974 — Phalangist and Palestinian forces clash

1975 — Civil war breaks out between Christians and Muslims

1976 — Syria sends thousands of troops to Lebanon; a cease-fire in the civil war is declared

1977 — Press censorship is imposed on all publications

1979 — The Chamber of Deputies is renamed the National Assembly

1981 — Israel bombs the PLO headquarters in Beirut

1982 — Israel invades Lebanon and occupies the entire area south of Beirut; president-elect Bashir Gemayal is assassinated; Amin Gemayal is elected president; PLO headquarters are moved from Beirut to Tunis, Tunisia

1983 — Terrorists bomb U.S. and French troop headquarters in Beirut killing 241 U.S. marines and 58 French troops; a 12-article agreement is signed declaring an end to hostilities; Conference of National Reconciliation is held in Geneva, Switzerland

1985 — Israel pulls out its combat troops from Lebanon, except for a security zone along the southern border; National Council of Tourism is reestablished; Lebanese Broadcasting Corporation is established

1986 — Palestinian forces attack settlements in northern Israel by rockets

1987 — Lebanese Prime Minister Rashid Karami is assassinated; Beirut airport is closed; air service to and from Beirut airport is suspended; some 8,000 Syrian troops move into Beirut area

1989 — Large scale fighting breaks out between Syrian and Christians in Beirut; the Taif Agreement comes into force

1990 — General Michel Aoun is evicted from the presidential palace; the greater Beirut Security Plan comes into effect; the Second Lebanese Republic is inaugurated

1991 — President Elias Hrawi signs a treaty with Syria; Christian, Druze, and Shiite militias turn over their armaments to the Lebanese army; Lebanese film director Maroun Bagdadi receives international award at the Cannes Film Festival; all remaining U.S. and British hostages held in Lebanon are released

1992 — Lebanon participates in Middle East peace conferences

IMPORTANT PEOPLE

Alexander the Great (356-323 B.C.), defeated Persians at the Battle of Issus in 333 B.C.

Marc Antony (82 or 81-30 B.C.), Roman general

Michel Aoun, Christian military leader; evicted in 1990 from the presidential palace that he occupied for 750 days; he was in exile in France in 1991

Yasser Arafat (1929-   ), chairman of the Palestine Liberation Organization (PLO)

Maroun Bagdadi, Lebanese film director who won Cannes Film Festival award in 1991 for his film *Hors de Vie (Out of Life)*

Bashir II (1767-1850), Druze leader from the Shihab family from southern Lebanon

Nabih Berri, Amal militia leader

Dany Chamoun (-1990), Christian politician, assassinated in October 1990

Camille Chamoun (1900-87), Lebanese president from 1952 to 58; he granted votes to women

Faud Chehab (1902-73), commander-in-chief of the Lebanese army; also Lebanese president from 1958 to 1964

Cleopatra (69-30 B.C.), queen of Egypt

Constantine (c.274-337), Roman emperor who saw a vision of the cross in the sky; founded the city of Byzantium (later Constantinople, now Istanbul in Turkey)

Charles Debbas, elected first president of Lebanon under the French Mandate

Emile Edde, president of Chamber of Deputies before Lebanon's independence

Esarhaddon (d.669 B.C.), Assyrian king who razed the city of Sidon to the ground

Sheikh Muhammad Hussein Fadlallah, spiritual mentor of the Hezbollah sect

Sulayman Franjiya (1910-   ), Lebanese president from 1970 to 1976

Gamel Abdel Nasser (1918-70), president of Egypt

Samir Geagea, Phalangist military leader

Amin Gemayel (1942-   ), Lebanese president from 1982 to 1988

Bachir Gemayel (1947-82), Lebanese president; assassinated in 1982

Pierre Gemayel (1905-84), founder and paramount leader of the Lebanese Phalangist organization

Khalil Gibran (1883-1931), also spelled Jibran, a native of Lebanon, internationally renowned for his paintings and literary work; best known work is the long poem *The Prophet*

Philip Habib, U.S. Middle East envoy of Lebanese ancestry

Saad Haddad, Lebanese army officer who declared an area of 700 sq. mi. (1,800 sq km) in southern Lebanon as independent free Lebanon in 1979

Charles Helou (1912-   ), Lebanese president from 1964 to 1970

Hiram (989-936 B.C.), king of Tyre from 969 to 936 B.C.

Salin al-Hoss, Dr. (1930-   ), Sunni Muslim, Lebanese prime minister from 1976 to 1980, and again from 1989 to 1990

Elias Hrawi, Maronite Christian, elected president in 1989

al-Hussain Hussaini, Lebanese president in 1991

Kamal Jumblatt (1917-77), Lebanese politician; father of Walid Jumblatt

Walid Jumblatt (1949-   ), Druze leader; also leader of the Progressive Socialist party

Juvenal, Roman writer who wrote about Lebanese immigrants in Rome

Abdul-Hamid Karami (1890-1947), Sunni Muslim and a major political figure in Lebanon

Omar Karami, Sunni Muslim; prime minister elected in 1990; brother of late prime minister Rashid Karami

Rashid Karami (1921-87), Sunni Muslim; ten times prime minister of Lebanon between 1956 and 1987

Bishara al-Khuri (1890-1964), Maronite, Lebanese president from 1943 to 1952

Emile Lahud, Lebanese army commander

Charles Habib Malik (1906-87), Lebanon's leading diplomat; also president of the 13th United Nations General Assembly

Rene Mouawad, Maronite Christian elected Lebanon's president in 1989; he was assassinated on the 17th day after his inauguration

Muawiyah (c.602-680), founder of Umayyad Dynasty

Muhammad (570-632), founder of Islam

al-Sadr Musa (1928-78), Shiite Muslim and a major political leader

Alfred Naccash, Greater Lebanon's president, appointed by the Vichy government

Nebuchadnezzar II (ruled 605 to 562 B.C.), a Babylonian king

Abu Nidal (1937-   ), one of the most elusive figures in contemporary Palestinian politics

Porphyry (c.224-c.305), Greek philosopher who published essays of Plotinus

Ptolemy (90-168), astronomer and geographer from Egypt

Saladin (1137 or 1138-93), Muslim general during the Crusades

Elias Sarkis, Lebanese president 1976 to 1982

Shahlin Shahlin, a peasant leader who demanded abolition of feudal (landowner) class

Georges Shehade, writer

Chafic-al Wazzan, Lebanese prime minister from 1976 to 1984

Looking down on Qadisha Valley from the Lebanon Mountains

INDEX

Page numbers that appear in boldface type indicate illustrations

About the Author

Leila Merrell Foster is a lawyer, United Methodist minister, and clinical psychologist with degrees from Northwestern University and Garrett Evangelical Theological Seminary. She is the author of books and articles on a variety of subjects.

Dr. Foster's love of travel began early as she listened to her mother and older sister read aloud travel and adventure stories. As a youngster, she enjoyed the family trips through which she learned geography, geology, history, art, agriculture, and economics in a very pleasant manner.

Dr. Foster also has written Enchantment of the World: *Bhutan, Iraq,* and *Jordan.*